On My Own Two Wheels

Naomi Cahen was born in 1986 and grew up by a lake in a bilingual home (French and English), where the plethora of objects have personalities. She currently lives and works in Lausanne, Switzerland, sometimes as an author, mostly as a designer and always as Autistic, advocating for neurodiversity whenever she can. She co-wrote the short film 'Action' with Benoît Monney which was nominated for the 2023 Swiss Film Awards.

Lynette Raven has a Master of Arts Degree in Translation, and she established Raven Translation Press in 2023. She worked in France and Switzerland for several years as a translator, interpreter, and teacher of English. She currently lives in Norfolk with her husband and Rollo the dog.

NAOMI CAHEN

On My Own Two Wheels

TRANSLATED FROM THE FRENCH BY

Lynette Raven

RAVEN TRANSLATION PRESS

Norwich

Published by Raven Translation Press 2024

Copyright © Naomi Cahen 2022
English translation copyright © Lynette Raven 2024

Illustrations © Naomi Cahen

All rights reserved.
No part of this publication may be reproduced, stored in a retrieval system, or transmitted, in any form or by any means, without the prior permission of the publisher.

First published with the title *Une chambre à air* in 2022
by Slatkine, Geneva

ISBN 978-1-0685400-0-4

To Poc and All The Missing Cats

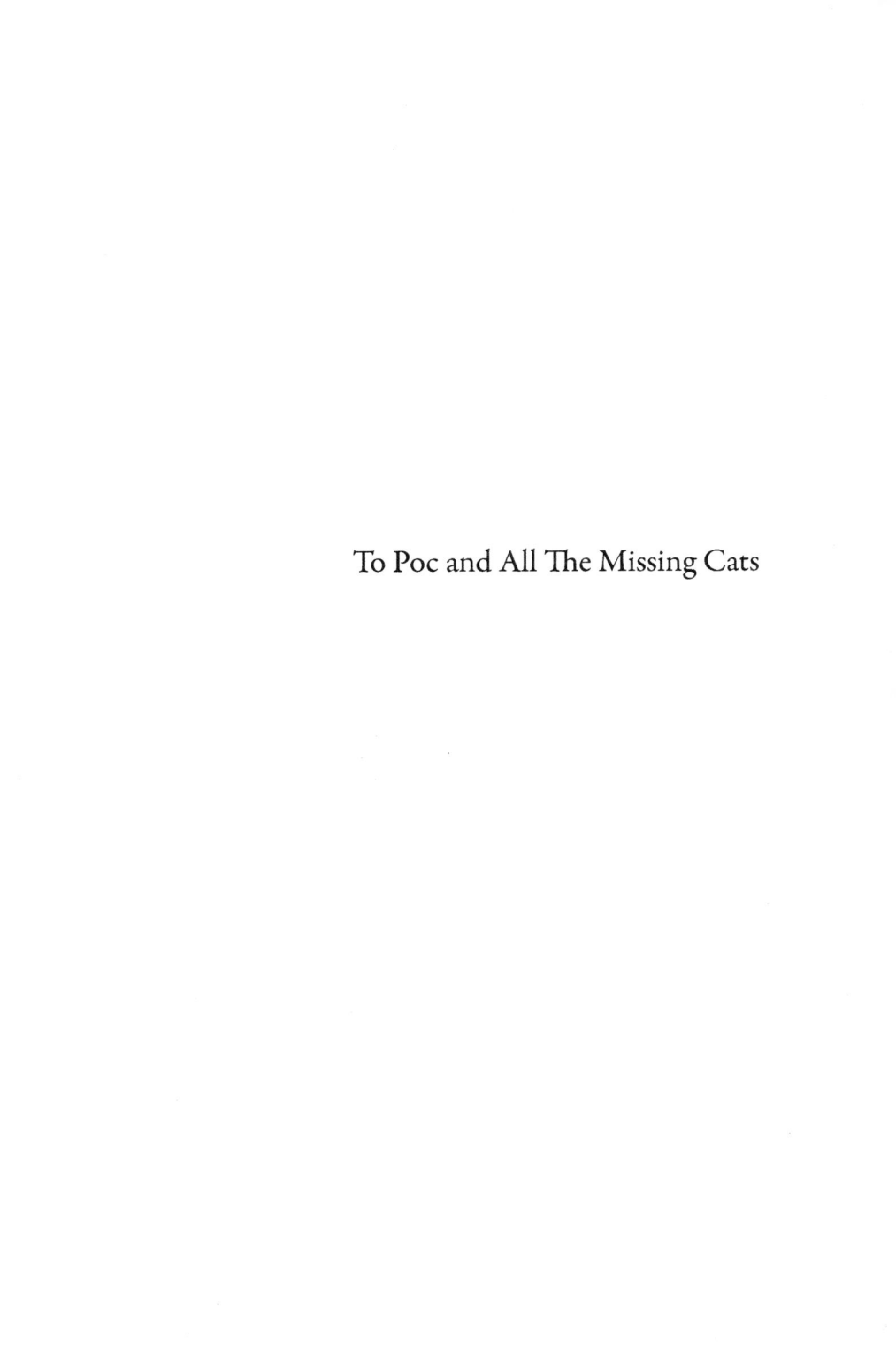

22nd September

Lausanne, Switzerland.
Alone at last. Well, to be honest, it's only been three days, so it's pushing it a bit to write that at this point. As though I've been waiting for this for ages. It's obviously everything I didn't want. All my existential phobia is nestled therein. In the idea of being alone. As an adolescent, I was obsessed with the dream of the perfect partner, the model man, Prince Charming – I know, it's sickening – and the pages of my personal diaries are full of the stuff. I did everything I could to avoid loneliness. I feel that most friendships are created remotely and are peppered with pretension and behaviour protocols, whereas the concept of a couple – more intimate – is the best way of making life rather less cold and prickly. We get up in the morning and there, at the very least, is the other person. We blend and merge into each other. We believe that love makes us grow but we add a cushion of fat to one another so we feel the outside world less. If our responsibilities become too much, there's our other half to lessen the burden, to snuggle up to and turn back time. Because everyone wants to go back to their childhood, don't they? To prolong it or change it, or both. That's what starting a family is all about.

When I was a teenager and realised I'd have to fly the nest one day, a phantasy* appeared that had been stashed under a heap of conventional thinking: I could be looked after. My concerned close friends and family could organise an American-style intervention – you're struggling, we're taking over – to put me in a kind of care home where I'd have a room with a glass door and a balcony overlooking the gardens and a bed with several positions depending on the degree of horizontality required for the inactivity of the hour. And they could provide me with a grabber to snatch objects out of my reach. I'd have everything I needed then: a bed to sleep in when the day is finally done, and we're all entitled to our daily death; meals served by the staff, so I don't have to make product choices (organic, in season, local, unprocessed, no additives, no packaging, etc.) nor decide on the menu, nor trouble myself with its preparation; and probably psychological and medical supervision, like regular visits to the doctor, and a workshop where we paint on the backs of table mats every Thursday afternoon in the canteen that has been temporarily transformed for the occasion. I would thus be confined to a life of restriction, free of this array of options. Basically, I admit that I've always had a slight penchant for avoiding life. 'Get me out of here.' The image of a video game addict comes to mind, with a virtual reality mask glued to their head and tubes driven into their body to keep them alive.

---

* The spelling 'fantasy' is much more common. I'd like to have the choice between 'ph' and 'f' for other words, like phantom. Fantom. But the 'ph' is a lot more enigmatic.

I longed to be passive. Probably because of the absurd unspoken thoughts I had, inspired by my grandmother's frequent stays in convalescent homes. I considered this notion with surprise and irony. It makes me chuckle to say I'd be happy in a psychiatric hospital, after the perfect childhood I had. A few years ago, whilst having a drink with my brother, he burst out laughing and confessed that he often had the same fantasy. And last week, a colleague in his early thirties told me he can't wait for the day when he can finally put his false teeth in a glass with a fizzy sterilising tablet. We joke about it. Kind of. There is something in it. I understand that life is too much. That if we could lighten the load and reduce the responsibility a bit, we would. There's too much information to take in, too many demands, too many ideals to pursue which contradict and clash with each other, and if you try to tackle the whole lot, you'll never set sail. So we choose what we keep and what we chuck away. Too much weight can hold us back, but an empty luggage trolley is free-wheeling folly.

I've stripped back a lot. So, yes. Alone at last. One man. Two men. Both with the same first name. Economical and disturbing at the same time. One break-up. Two break-ups. No more men.

A riddle

My first is the Scots for mountain,
Dependable, solid, and strong.
My second's a film or book type
Where darkness and menace belong.
Name this genre where everyone dies,
And with my first, it's the name of two guys.

Upon leaving the second man, the first one becomes important again. We reassure each other. Just like before. My Inner Judge hovers and casts its shadow, growling.

> IJ: You leave the first one for the second one, then you leave the second one and cuddle up to the first one? You're evil. But you know that.
> Me: I'm not cuddling up and you're far too simplistic! In contrast to you, who's just made up of standardised and superficial principles, I am human. You're attacking my love life in a crude way, in the first degree, as if you're not familiar with my inner meanderings.
> IJ: Silence! Aren't you ashamed?
> Me: Yes, of course I am.
> IJ. You're playing with the first one, just like the second one played with you!
> Me: I'm not playing at all. I'm not like that. It's natural to need other people!
> IJ: But it's not natural to *need* other people.
> Me: That's exactly what the second one thought... And he'll always be sad and lonely.

To understand what's happening to me and what is yet to come, I look up the stages of grief by Googling 'stages of grief'. As it would appear that a break-up counts as a form of grief.

1. Shock
2. Denial
3. Anger

4. Fear
5. Negotiation
6. Depression
7. Sadness
8. Acceptance
9. Forgiveness
10. Looking for meaning
11. Serenity

Today is my third day, post break-up, and I already feel I'm at stage 10, looking for meaning. But that's not possible! Not so fast! There must be some mistake. Two days ago, I didn't think I'd ever get over it – the pain went right through me. But it does feel as though I've gone through all those stages. Can they really last just a few hours? Can the order jump about? Should I expect whiplash and high-speed reversing? Could I really have climbed such high mountains and come back down again? Are there secret passages and bridges between stages? Perhaps going from the first guy, let's call him B1, to the second, who shall be known as B2, means the two break-ups, just six months apart, have teamed up and shared the workload, giving me a '2-in-1' experience.

There must be some correlation to be made between the intensity and rapidity of falling for someone, the length of the relationship itself, and the healing period. Perhaps there's even a formula to be found. Perhaps it already exists. Is it that the more intense and rapid the falling in love is, the shorter the relationship, and the more painful the healing process, but speeded up?

To learn how to move on, you probably have to move on. To learn how to be alone, you probably have to be alone. I know how to ride a bike. That's one thing I already do know how to do. So pursuing these three things at the same time – moving on, alone, on a bike – could be the way to go.

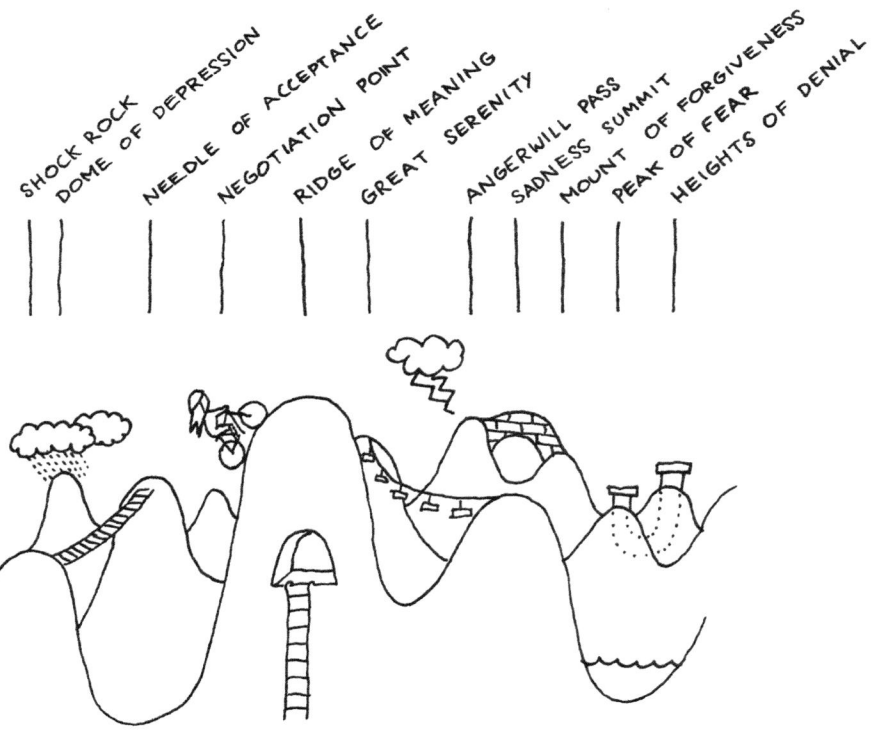

23rd September

Equipped with new feelings of elation, I ring the bike shop in England and explain that I want to ride to Lausanne, Switzerland, pedalling all the way from their London branch. I was hoping to get comprehensive answers on everything I would need: the best type of wheels for my adventure, the lightest and strongest material there is for the frame, the perfect shape of handlebars for my arms, and advice on what saddle to buy for my size and weight. 'People of your build generally have rather angular buttocks, so you'll need a G3-20 saddle. It'll be a real treat for your bum.'

I had imagined they'd really take care of me, just like in that psychiatric hospital, that I could get on the phone and say, 'Hello, I don't know anything, tell me everything, and I'll buy!' Of course, the Englishman on the other end of the line is befuddled by this undemanding customer. There's no resistance whatsoever on my part – I swallow everything he says. When I ask him what type of brakes I need, discs or pads, he tells me that it's up to me to do the research because it's a very personal choice. Obviously, I feel guilty and confess that I'm a complete novice. But, deep inside, I'm irritated. I need a bit of decisiveness from this expert. I want him to give me a lecture on the subject! I want him to say, 'What you need is this bike here. I can see the type of person you are, I understand your expectations, they're the same as mine, so let me put together the ultimate bike for you that you'll never want to be without.' Because isn't he there precisely to spare me the bother of drumming up interest in tiresome things like the mechanics of a bicycle? It can't be that difficult, but it would mean embarking on a whole new world, where I'd have to learn everything, read everything, know everything. And I must admit that something about it bores me senseless. My arms have only just got sufficient energy to hang at my sides these days. I've already got enough going on in my head, more than enough actually, meaning I struggle* to keep it all in order.

---

* To struggle. The multitude of consonants colliding with each other paint a sound picture of this difficulty.

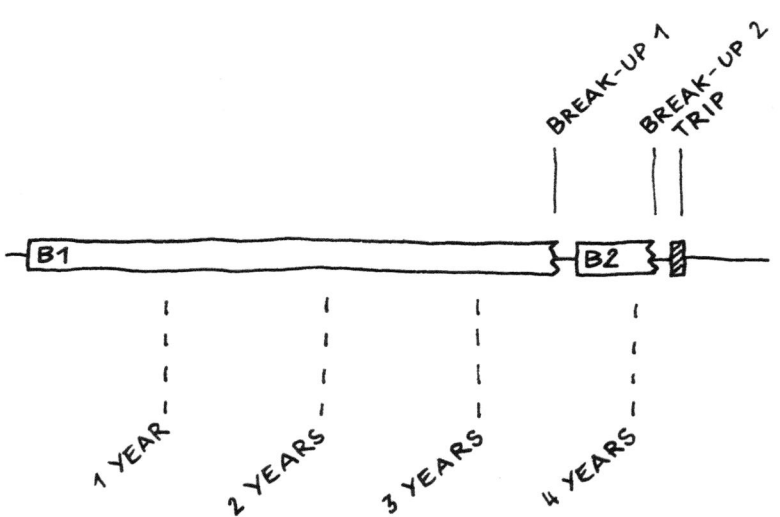

THE B-TIMELINE

24th September

It's morning. Everything is starting again. Like snippets of shameful echoes that resurface after an evening's drinking, I remember I've officially announced to my family and friends that I'm going to do this bike trip. The trip that has been wooing me for several years now. I can feel the weight of my words on my forehead. My eyebrows are collapsing. The world is no longer the place of theoretical game-playing that had me so fired-up yesterday. Today, the world is hostile, too vast, and no-one knows me. No-one gives a damn. A kind of existential agoraphobia.

There's a painful emptiness in the hollow I've got inside me, a bit like hunger. And everything is swirling around it like a hurricane. Sadness spits from the hole. It's verging on nausea. I have become a naked steel structure, and the coldness of my own metallic matter is burning me. I am so cold at the thought of the adventure ahead. But luckily my fridge is full. I can try and pad out my heart, at least.

I don't really know why this fear overwhelms me to such an extent. Perhaps if I could explain it to myself, it would dissipate. Nothing is ready for this trip, I'm risking everything, everything needs a kick-start, and nobody is going to do it for me. All paths are possible, but I won't know if I've made the right choice until I'm in the choice. I'm inevitably getting closer to my trip, but the unknown remains – fuzzy and frightening.

When I'm on the website looking for my future bike, I have no idea what to go for anymore. I note from the photo that the gear levers are positioned at the very ends of the handlebars, like a crown of pointed horns with little thingummies attached to them (fig. 3). I know that on most bikes, these controls are located on the brake handles (fig. 1), and that on some old bicycles, they're found on the diagonal strut of the tubular frame, resembling the more-or-less attentive ears of a hare (fig. 2). I've never seen such a configuration and I firmly believe that if someone had told me the levers could be perched on the front end of the saddle, I'd have believed them (fig. 4). Just goes to show how much I know.

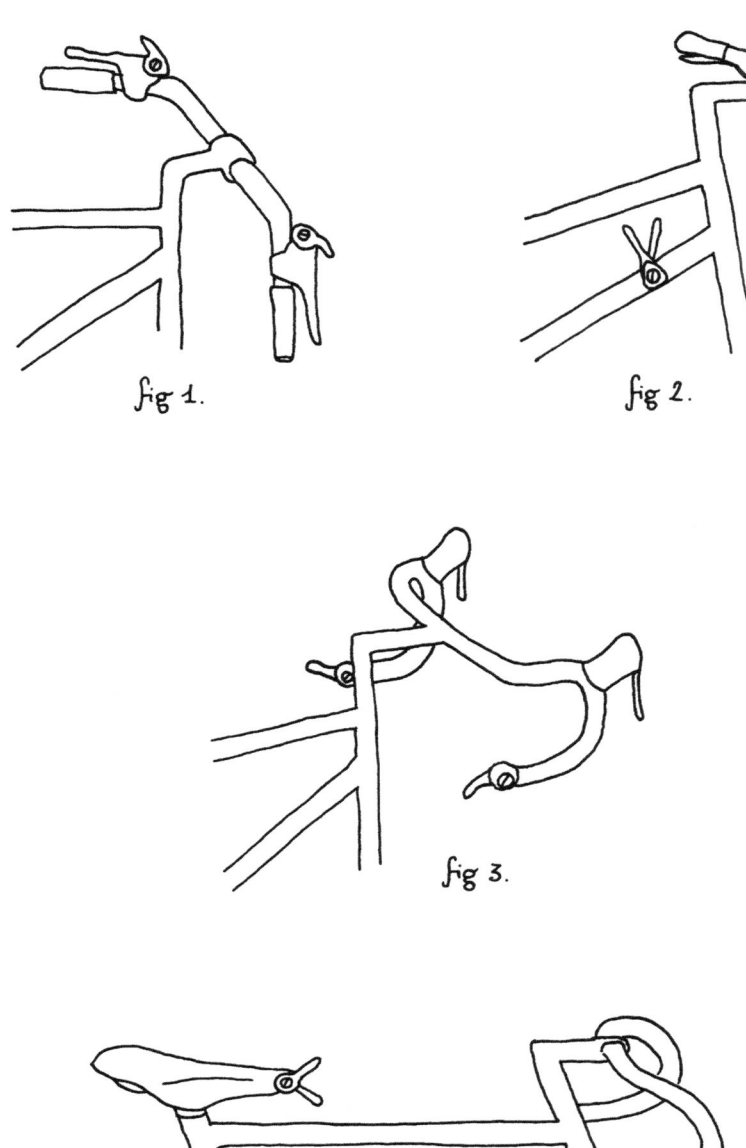

25th September

And then there's the Internet with everything. No wonder I'm thrown into confusion. I read a few things about gears and how they work. But the more I read, the more questions I have, and the more debates I find between various systems striving to convince rival camps. I learn there are gear levers that work by friction or indexing. From what I've read, and without testing the mechanics, I discover that, with indexed shifters, the small lever stops at precise notches that correspond with the gears but where friction levers are concerned, how you engage the desired gear depends on how far you push or pull this lever. I understand that the latter, more refined, system is practical as it would withstand the mechanical parts slackening over time. Especially over 1000 kilometres. Obviously, it's all about physics and everything is destined to crumble.

My biggest fear is getting it wrong. Choosing the wrong route, the one that's not rural or picturesque; taking the wrong clothes with me, the ones that don't keep me warm; staying at the wrong B&Bs, the ones where I feel alone and ridiculous. I'm scared of getting home and telling myself I spent all my money on that wrong trip. In this petrified state, I draw up a list to stop myself from thinking about it too much. Everything becomes possible when you break it down. I need to organise the organisation of my trip:

1. Order the bike on the website.
2. Organise the outbound journey: decide on my date of arrival in London and the date I'll collect the bike.
3. Choose the stages of my return trip: the itinerary.
4. Decide what to pack in my bags.

It's reassuring to segment everything. Once I'm on the road, I'll be less scared because I'll be there. But at this moment in time, even the phone call I've got to make to Noah, the English chap at the bike shop, terrifies me. Me, who's nervous the day before going snowshoe hiking with a girlfriend because of the different times involved (wake up at 07:00, train departs at 08:12, arrives at 09:28, bus at 09:45, arrives in the high mountains at 10:21) and the list of necessary kit, and who is actually relieved when such plans are cancelled. I have to face facts – I haven't chosen the project that sits most comfortably with me. I'd like to be able to take all the comfort of home and catapult myself outside with it. In a bubble. Safe. In my open-air bedroom.

Being an adult and doing things is a role we take on. Perhaps it doesn't come naturally to any of us. It's the 'I can do everything, and I have the right to be me' mindset. In short, I can and I am. But it's one of those days where I'm suspended from my life instead of riding it. I'm not in control of anything. I'm dangling, my arms are clinging on, my grip is tight, but my biceps are incapable of lifting me up. My legs are hanging just as helplessly, in spite of their strength, because they're too far from the ground. So I advance as best I can, sliding my hands along the cable, my shoulders slightly dislocated by my weight. If I decided to have a bit of fun, if I gained some momentum and got up some swing, maybe I'd manage to get back on top.

26th September

I've purchased the bike. Chased it down and pur*chased* it. There's no going back. Metal parts assembled in the shape of a bicycle exist and are intended for me. They're in London and I can go and fetch them on the 9th of October. I therefore decide to arrive on the 8th, and on the 10th I'll start devouring my first pedal-powered miles. I don't want to hang around in the capital, pretending to be interested in anything else.

I plunge myself into preparation for this ride, as though into dark water laden with particles. In contrast to my *Lac Léman**, this water is stifling and sucks me down further. I think about it constantly. When I'm in bed at night, several hours of anguish tick by before

---

* *Léman* is the lake that I live beside. It is half Swiss and half French. Its name is of Indo-European descent and means 'lake'. People call it different names, depending on where they live. Here in Lausanne, we call it *Lac Léman* which is a total tautology as *lac* and *léman* mean the same thing. But the term has been used both here and in France since ancient times (*lemanè limnè* then *lacus lemanus*). In Geneva, however, they like to call it *Lac de Genève* – Lake Geneva, which has become its official name in the English language. But I think such a large body of water, that's been around far longer than any of our cities, should be entitled to its own name. And, lastly, my English grandmother calls it 'Lemon Lake'.

I'm released. Then, in the blink of a wet eyelash, I'm up again, continuing my research. I'm terrified that the fateful date will arrive too soon and that I won't have had time to complete the preparation. And when it comes to getting ready, I freeze. I'm scared of the cold that's coming and I'm cold with the fear that has already set in. I hope the sun will occasionally make an appearance and ignite it all, that the leaves will catch fire and then carpet my way ahead.

In my current state of mind, I begin to doubt this out-of-my-comfort-zone adventure story. I'll have nothing to say. I'll be digging infertile ground. There's the fear of no longer believing in it, of letting a spark die. The spark of the written word. The spark of the journey. But I know that unless I get injured, I won't give up on my pedalling. Has this trip become nothing but a challenge I've got to meet? That's a bit sterile. I wouldn't want to do all this just because of other people's recommendations, expectations, or opinions. That's not enough for me. But I am feeling some social pressure. If I lived alone in the world, would I be undertaking this adventure?

I was waiting for some free time to come along this summer, like a clearing in my work jungle. I was waiting for the space to finally explore this strange, ultra-intense relationship I was experiencing with B2. I was waiting for us to get in sync so that we could go away for a few days and domesticate each other. I was dreaming of being together quietly, with no commitments, just the two of us. It had been his idea, after all.

Then the weeks went by, and I could see these plans falling apart without me even touching them. I asked him to help me understand, but he thought I was being confrontational. B2 finally admitted that he would have liked me to do my bike trip – which was still at the embryo stage – before going away with him. He felt that I needed to fulfil myself more first, and to correct certain parts of me, even just to be with him. I believed in his sudden show of benevolence and was caught in his honey trap. I moved towards him: he slipped away. I retreated: he invaded. According to B2, it was because I hadn't worked on myself enough that we hadn't been able to build a relationship. The separation had basically been a way of telling him, 'I don't buy into you anymore, I'm no longer trying to figure you out.' After his relentless harassment – 'Do your own thing, be yourself!' – I forget that I've got it, this thing, and what I am. A few days after the break-up, now silence has returned, I can hear the trip getting back on its feet and it calls to the very heart of me.

27th September

My computer seems to be having a meltdown, probably because of all the TextEdit windows I've got open on my desktop. It takes ten minutes to load a single page and struggles to cope with all the information I've thrown at it.

I've noted down handy links, relevant blogs, potential stopovers, a few ideas of possible routes, a list of equipment, clothing, uncertainties, things I still need to buy, still need to organise, things I still need to add to a list, lists I still need to make, and the list of miscellaneous things that will nonetheless need to be dealt with in the time I've got left.

At this point, I just need to get it all out. But these windows are crowding in on me, along with all the Firefox ones which each contain at least 28 tabs. Like computer, like user. So I try to declutter my screen a bit, in the hope of decontaminating my visual environment.

I'm starting to get a vague idea of the route I'm going to take. The cycle path websites aren't up to date. It's a real piece-by-piece archaeological reconstruction. Am being slowed down in my search by the thought that the perfect website is out there. Probably the same with men. I find it astonishing that this ideal website doesn't exist yet and instead of accepting the fact and patiently gathering the information I need, I'm raging inside at this messy jumble and keep on faffing.*

I'm convinced that once I find this dream site, I'll get back all the time and energy I've wasted looking for it. What I want is one website with a map of Europe – of the world, even – where all the official cycle paths, greenways and *véloroutes* are brought together in one place. All the distances would be available at the click of a mouse, you could hover the cursor over gradients to see all the ups and downs, plus the type of surface, and how challenging it is to cycle on. You'd even be able to see potential stopovers and their unique points of interest, as well as reviews from previous visitors (although, to be honest, I couldn't care less). It would be possible to build your own route and calculate distances. This whole concept both excites and depresses me – I'm such a product of my generation.

But it's fun to play around with finding my way. Even if I feel like I have to pull the needle of my route out of this internet haystack, there's a chance that the perfect itinerary is out there, and I've got to track it down. The perfect site, the perfect route, the perfect man... I want to find it all, and I want it all to be perfect. No surprise

---

* Such an odd word, just a sound really. You can practically hear its meaning. 'Stop faffing around!' It also makes me think of the French verb *farfouiller* which I love because I picture a crazy cartoon character in a blind panic with droplets of sweat emanating from them. The word implies it's not an entirely serious search. There's a waste of energy, a hint of madness, and even anger about it.

I'm in a panic. While talking to B1, who's interested in my trip, he takes three minutes to locate useful websites that it would take me three hours to root out. I'm blown this way and that, trying to find everything but losing myself in it all. Great approach.

I did manage to book my flight, though. I leave on Tuesday 8th October. Then, after London, I'll probably go to Newhaven, on the English Channel coast, and take the ferry to Dieppe. From there, I'll go to Saint-Valéry-sur-Somme, still on the coast, and take the number 30 *véloroute* to push inland as far as the Marne. My only concern is that it seems this cycle path isn't entirely finished. Difficult to tell, as none of the websites is particularly current. After digging around, I discover they're going to update the map of France on the 26th of September. So... yesterday! But it's impossible to lay my hands on it. When I leave the Marne *département*, I'll have to follow the V52 for a while, up to Vitry-le-François, then the V53 until Heuilley-sur-Saône. Then it all gets a bit hazy. I could go through Besançon (or Dôle) and cross the Jura, passing through Pontarlier, or make a detour and go through Geneva. I prefer the thought of the Jura, even though it'll be a bit of a climb. I just think of the descent.

I'd like to try and convince a few girlfriends to join me for some of the way. Towards the end, probably. But it could be tricky – most of them have no bike and too many children.

As I scroll through north-eastern France, with my finger on its little scooter, I come across some amusing clumps of letters: La Ferté-sous-Jouarre, Revigny-sur-

Ornain, Louan-Villegruis-Fontaine, which all sound suspiciously too French to be real. You get a sense of the amalgamation of territories, political compromises, and the distant past.

Poem in French
(to be read aloud)

Touffreville-la-Corbeline, ①
   Yvré-le-Pôlin. ②
Gesvres-le-Chapitre, Outines, ③   ④
   Baboeuf, Bains-les-Bains. ⑤   ⑥

Anchenoncourt-et-Chazel, ⑦
   Piblange et Soupir. ⑧   ⑨
Bû, Domrémy-la-Pucelle, ⑩ ⑪
   Knutange et Courcuire. ⑫   ⑬

Sy, Chatonrupt-Sommermont, ⑭ ⑮
   Fère-en-Tardenois. ⑯
Boué, Cussey-sur-l'Ognon, ⑰   ⑱
   Vitry-le-François. ⑲

Boucheporn, Sons-et-Ronchères, ⑳   ㉑
   Pruillé-l'Éguillé. ㉒
La Pot'rie-Cap-d'Antifer, ㉓
   Souligné-Flacé. ㉔

Berck, Bosc-Roger-sur-Buchy, ㉕   ㉖
   Trécon, Gratibus. ㉗   ㉘
Pissy, Le Plessis-Placy, ㉙   ㉚
   Fluquières et Farbus. ㉛   ㉜

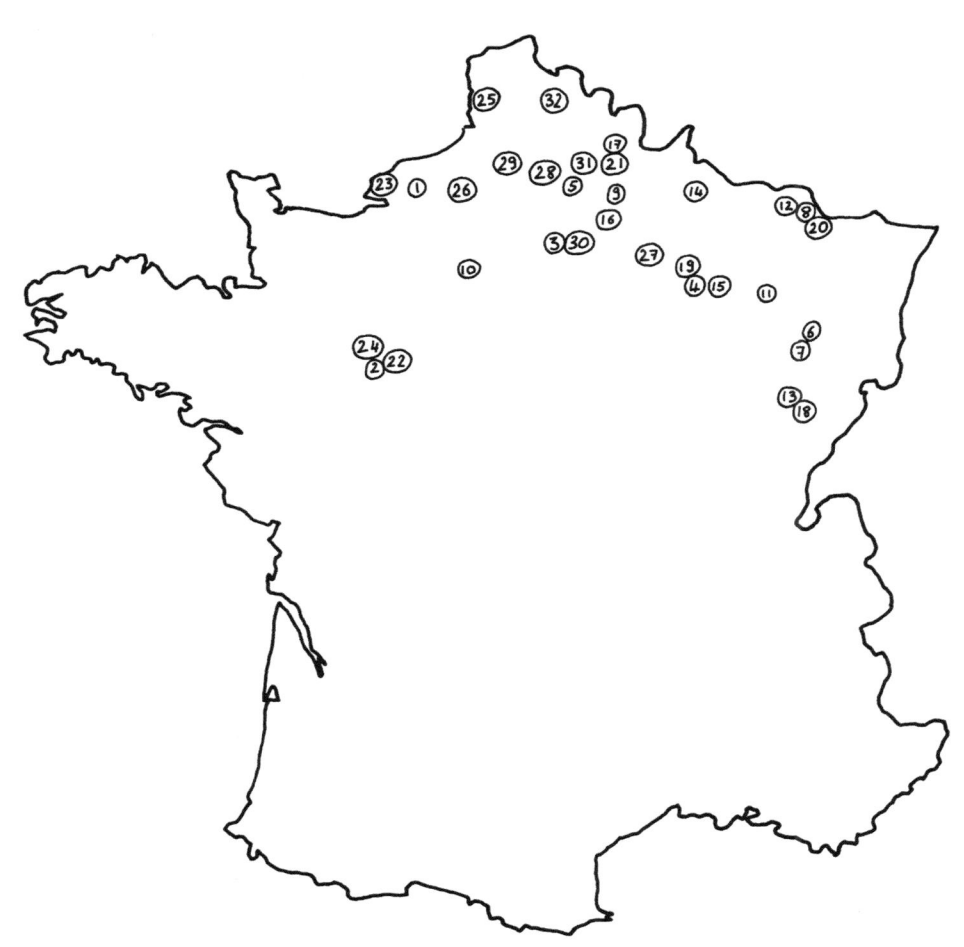

A week ago (a couple of days after the break-up), it was as though I'd moved on to other things. I no longer thought about B2, and the rare after-tastes of him disgusted me. As for B1, he left me indifferent. I was armour-plated. Since then, I've gone through every kind of state. I now have no surface, no skin. And I don't know if it's a man I miss or if it's the thought of this trip that intensifies my nakedness. I'm relying more and more heavily on TV shows. Fatty and sugary. On fags, too. Dry and ashy. I wonder which addiction will be the hardest to give up.

I think about this diary I'm writing and feel a bit embarrassed. Slightly ashamed to type my little words on my little laptop as if I were doing something worthwhile. I'd like to sharpen my writing, make it denser, whittle it down, and whip it up so it remains light. It's hard not to write everything that comes into my head, because it's very noisy. I have to make myself stop, lower my gaze, and look inwards, stay still so I can listen to what comes into this space. There's always something, however small. Sometimes just micro-crumbs that are barely big enough to bite on. If I put morsels of edible ideas together, does that mean I'm creating a slice of thought to sink my teeth into? An assortment of several good ingredients doesn't necessarily make a good cake.

Anyway, back to reality. Looking at cycle routes online, some of them are so fragmented that I wonder if they're worth the detour or whether the site's algorithm is just useless. I've bought a tiny aluminium box of solid toothpaste for the journey. Plus a small amount of solid shampoo, and a bar of Marseille soap that I'll use for washing both myself and my clothes. Consume more to consume less...

28th September

Planning my itinerary is taking a lot longer than expected. I've found the exact route to follow, practically down to the last side street, on a greenway between London and Newhaven, but the part after Dieppe is less clear. It would appear that some of the sections are closed, or 'non-open', as it says on the map legends. None of the sites gives the same information.

Since deciding to do this trip, I've split myself in two. I spend half the day searching for my route, understanding websites, and demystifying my own project, and the other half losing myself in a television series. There is some satisfaction to be had in slowly discovering pieces of a puzzle that I am creating. Nothing is out of place.

When I'm bingeing on a series, everything around me is muted, everything is blurred, but not soft. Everything is distant and unreal. I no longer feel much, and no longer know anything. I forget how human relationships work. I forget the outside and don't listen to the inside. I ask myself exactly where I'm at.

The trip is, as usual for me, accompanied by the man of the moment and consists of a kind of hermetic and nebulous catapulting beyond commonly-accepted boundaries. I might have travelled to another continent – I can see there are differences: smells, colours, the sound of people – but I don't really believe it. My brain doesn't get it. It's a huge, orchestrated spectacle. A *Truman Show*. Everything moves with me, nothing is clear and straightforward. Like being drunk. A bubble. All contact through my senses is interrupted, disconnected, a layer of Vaseline over my eyes. But I can tell it's not normal. Other human beings seem to understand the experience of such a trip and even to enjoy it.

When we split up, after nearly four years of living together, B1 went off alone on the Trans-Siberian Railway for six weeks. A few friends joined him at different intervals to break up his journey. He then moved to London for work. He's still there but plans to return in the coming weeks. We've stayed in regular contact. I spend a lot of time texting him these days. Sometimes we phone each other. We want the relationship to be transparent and unambiguous. I don't know if that's possible. He said everything was clear to him, which is a relief. What haunts me most is the thought that I hurt him. Being tormented by that, I delayed our break-up for a long time. But B2 was encroaching too much on my life, and I could no longer ignore him. The split from B1 was like being sick after spending hours in bed, in denial.

Suddenly, I experience a twinge of sadness at the thought that B1 is no longer in love with me. I left him – I know I don't have the right to this twinge. But it's there all the same. Along with my Inner Judge…

Me: A twinge of sadness doesn't care whether it has the right to be there or not.
IJ: This twinge is the reaction of a child who's spoilt rotten, who wants to have her cake and to eat it, too, along with every cake in the bakery, all with a cherry on top.
Me: It's so easy to beat oneself up like that!
IJ: Because it's true...
Me: No, it's not! It's relying on normalised opinions shaped by a society that watches too many TV series...
IJ: Like you!
Me: ...where the characters act out formulaic performances that have been designed to convey simplistic, two-dimensional emotions. My twinge is there because I'm just not enough for me, and I need external proof of interest

It's been decided that B1 will cycle with me on the first two or three days, from London to Newhaven. I'm so relieved. B1 acts as a remarkable sticking-plaster solution to fear. And I know that nothing will happen between us because I don't want it to. The times that I do want it to are similar to a kind of love that resembles lazy loneliness. Loving him completely would make my life so much easier and more beautiful. But I don't think that would be my life. My life now is about stripping myself bare, lying down naked on the ice to understand my pain and its contours. Perhaps, once I've understood what's happening to me, once I've started cycling, I'll be

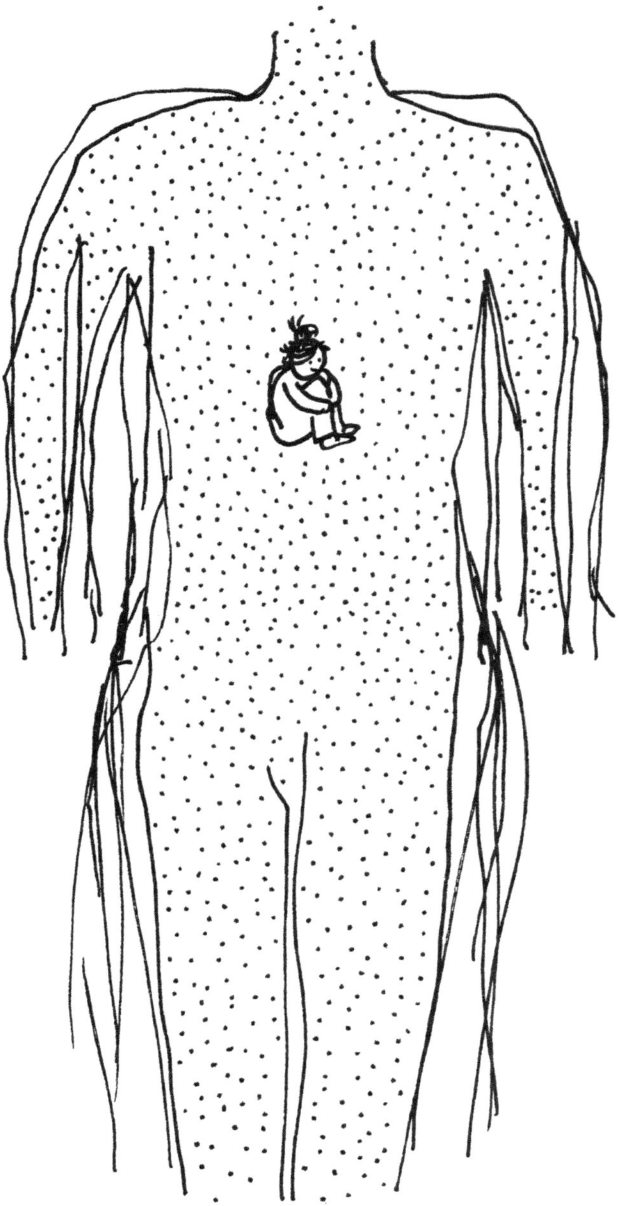

able to create a space inside me. A space to catch my breath when the outside is suffocating me, to come to terms with the world, shake up my thoughts, and devise a 'me' that makes sense.

My TV series keep me warm for one episode. Then the next. Then the next. And when it all stops – the series, the evening, the connection – everything falls apart. It all comes crashing down, everything in the same place as before. Nothing has changed, nothing has been sorted. Nothing has been considered, nothing has been listened to. I would like a series, a fag, and a B2, too.

A haze of fat, smoke, and dopamine. I think it's the first time I've really felt my veins crackle. All I had to do was think about him. Your whole life you point at something wonderful in the distance. You say, 'Look over there at that wonderful thing,' but no-one can see what you're talking about. So you calm down a bit and try to keep this wonderful thing to yourself so that you almost don't believe in it anymore. That's when you meet someone who can also see this far-off, wonderful thing. And you talk about it together, you're both ecstatic. Then, this person slowly reveals that you've imagined this wonderful thing, that you must have misunderstood what they could see in the distance. It wasn't that at all. You must be a bit weird. This person was B2.

I left him out of survival instinct. On the surface, he seemed like a nice guy, but very self-absorbed. He exposed my faults and brandished his solutions. I had never been pulled about so much. Everything was classed as a problem waiting to be solved. A kind of

Doctor Knock* with a messiah complex. He questioned everything and wanted to dig deeper than rock-bottom. I think that searching for such a degree of purity means he'll always be on the outside of everything. I wondered aloud if he was manipulating me. Sometimes he'd reply that he was, just as I was manipulating him, and that everything affected everything else. Other times he protested he wasn't, and that I could not be manipulated. That if I was being pushed around by him, I was the one who should have my head examined because I was allowing myself to be treated that way. His manipulation was so finely tuned and well-conceived that it could almost be considered a work of art. Master manipulator. I told him, 'You're crazy, you think humanity is too weak for you!' He responded with such a gentle laugh and such well-crafted arguments that I dissolved. One day, when I explained the feeling of being in love, he told me it was something he'd never want.

---

* *Knock* is a play from the 1920s by Jules Romain (often read at school in French-speaking countries) which recounts the arrival of a new doctor – Knock – in the old, unprofitable medical practice of a small town. By determining the inhabitants' wealth and implementing free consultations once a week, he manages to attract many patients and convince them that *'Les gens bien portants sont des malades qui s'ignorent'* ('People in good health are actually ill but don't know it yet'). When I read that as a teenager and wrote my school assignment on the play, I portrayed him as a brilliant doctor who had the rare ability to detect illnesses that other professionals couldn't. It was a story of hope, talent and generosity. When I enthusiastically shared my thoughts with my dad, he immediately said, 'Oh no, sweetie, you've got it the wrong way round – this guy's a charlatan! He's only trying to gain money and power!' I was so shocked and disappointed. I rewrote my essay, my eyes slightly widened.

29th September

I'll be leaving in nine days' time, and I still haven't told everyone close to me. Information circulates in a rather spasmodic way in our family. We spare certain people that we deem to be too sensitive, we forget to mention obvious things, such as going on holiday, hospital stays, and weddings. But I don't see why you should have to tell everybody everything. Even though I know she won't approve, I decide to phone my ninety-year-old great-aunt – let's call her Ninn – to tell her my news, because she's a person that I love and respect, and I know she'll want to know where I am for the next month. She's a very lonely, bright woman who doesn't change her mind easily. I sit for a moment on the edge of my bed before pressing the 'call' button. I breathe in and out, but my lungs don't seem convinced. I hope to catch her on a good day. I put my left middle finger on top of my left index finger and hold it there. Then my right index finger taps the screen to start the call.

She answers after ten rings with her post-war *'Voilà?'*, anxious and out-of-breath. She's reassured and happy to hear my voice. How do I broach the subject? I try and tell her about my life. My break-up with B2 ten days ago, and this new solitude. I'd like her to give me some good advice. Great words of wisdom from a ninety-year-old single, wise woman. But she asks me about work instead, wanting to make sure I've got some. My life must worry her because I don't have a salaried job, I earn money intermittently and work for myself. I jump straight in and tell her in one breath: 'Ninn, I'm going away for three weeks on a cycling trip. I've already bought the bike, which is in London, so I'm going to collect it on the 9th of October, and I'll ride it back. I should be home around the...' But she interrupts me. 'On your own?! On a bike? You're not serious. Naomi, you can't.' It's a stronger reaction than I was expecting. 'Yes, Ninn, but you don't have to worry. I've planned the whole journey. I'll cycle on car-free routes and I'll stay overnight with people who let out rooms.' Deathly silence. Shock. Then she lets out a horrified 'But!' She doesn't understand that I want to go it alone. We're on the phone for two hours as I try everything to reassure her. Her anxiety only increases my own. I talk to her as though she's a friend; I break through the generation barrier, I let her know it saddens me to hear she's entirely against my plans, but I've made up my mind and I'm going to do it. After one hundred and twenty-seven minutes and sixteen seconds without the slightest amount of progress, we both abandon our attempts at persuasion and hang up helplessly. Am wrung out.

Less than an hour later, I find myself curled up in a ball, suffering from a bout of the stomach pain I sometimes get. As usual, the attack lasts about seven hours. No sooner have I emerged from my ordeal

– it's 10 p.m. and my brain has finally got its plasticity back – than the phone rings. It's Ninn. Knowing that she routinely goes to bed at 8.30 every night, I imagine the worst and answer immediately. She apologises for the late call but she's so worried that she couldn't help herself. She begs me not to go through with the trip and suggests other options. She seems convinced I'm hurtling towards my death. She's shocked that people are supporting me in these plans, and that my parents and brother haven't put a stop to this crazy idea. I reply that they can't pass judgment on the decisions I make but that their support is invaluable to me, and I would really like to have hers. I suggest ringing her every three days during my trip. She refuses straightaway. 'That would be even worse!' she says. Her fear is at the helm and she's no match for it.

30th September

I'm making very slow progress with my preparation, although I work on it constantly. When Giusy rings, I don't know whether to answer. I know she's phoning to talk about the final stages in the Jura that we want to do together. I answer the call anyway, suspecting she'll take me for a bungling bike-tripper. I tell her I'm scared out of my wits. She's a kind and sympathetic listener despite the human bulldozer she's always been. She gives me straightforward, concrete advice that wraps warmth around my heart.

I then go to my brother's, and he lends me two cycle bags, a Swiss Army knife, an iPhone charger, two iPhone cases (one with touch-sensitive protection in case of rain, the other without), a cashmere jumper, and two merino T-shirts. I know that tight-fitting clothing won't be an option as comfort is paramount in such a potentially uncomfortable project. If I'd had to buy all that, it would have cost me 700 Swiss francs, easy. Whilst we practise changing the inner tube on his Brompton, he gives me the same reassuring advice as Giusy.

I feel that (nearly all) my friends and family support me, they're excited by my trip, they get it, and they're a bit envious of me. Personally, I'm not that envious of me but I believe it's the connection I have with these people that helps me move forward. I still don't know what I want to prove, nor to whom.

1st October

By organising this trip, I'm learning to organise this trip. People I know are equipped with a useful sense of logic. They know that to cycle from London to Lausanne, you need:

1. to be in London
2. to own a bike
3. to get to the right places by riding said bike
4. to sleep
5. to eat
6. to get dressed.

In other words:

1. to go to London
2. to buy the bike (tick!)
3. a way to find your bearings and to reach your various destinations
4. B&Bs with vacancies for every night
5. something to eat
6. something to wear.

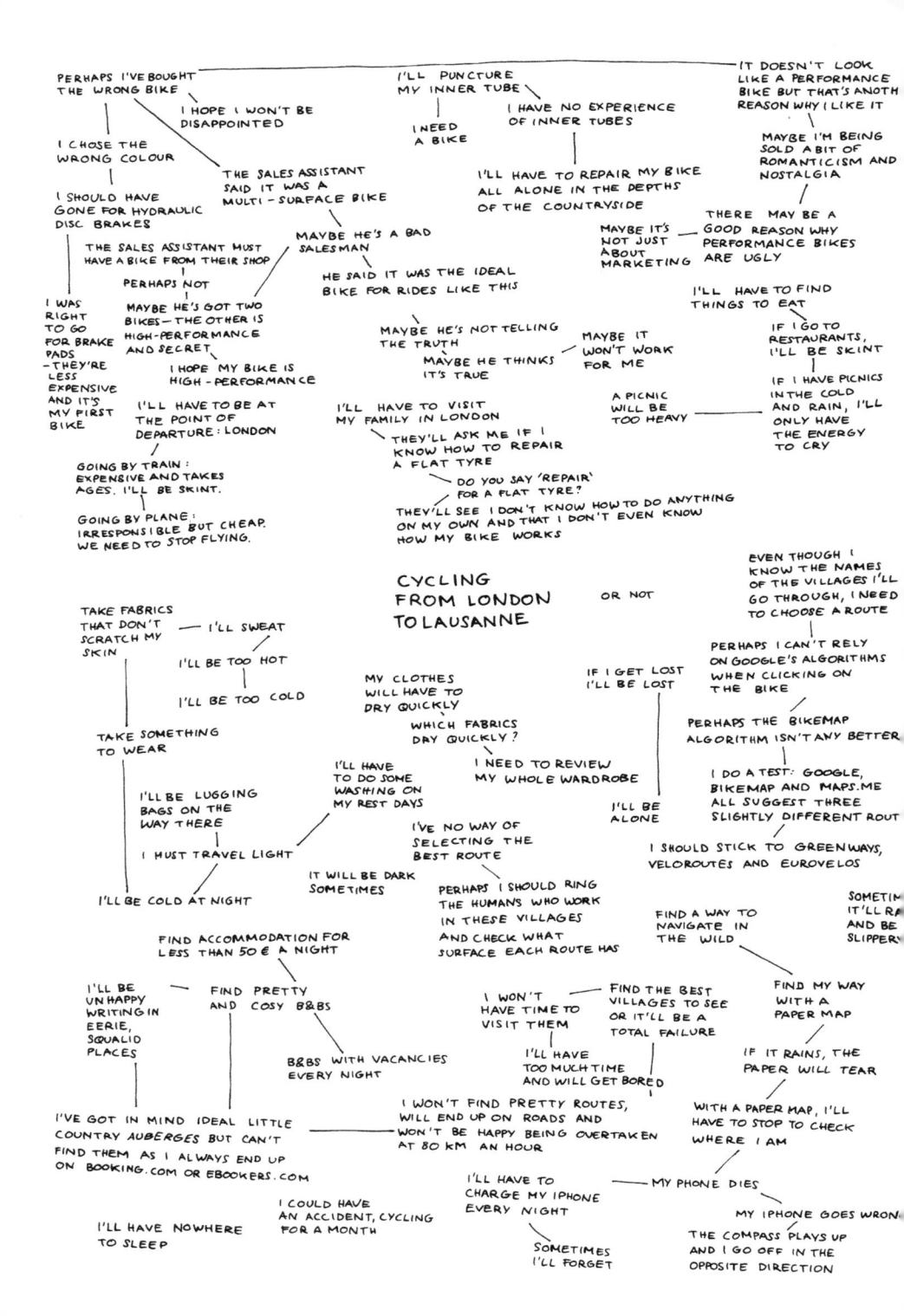

CYCLING FROM LONDON TO LAUSANNE

OR NOT

- PERHAPS I'VE BOUGHT THE WRONG BIKE
  - I HOPE I WON'T BE DISAPPOINTED
  - I CHOSE THE WRONG COLOUR
  - I SHOULD HAVE GONE FOR HYDRAULIC DISC BRAKES
    - THE SALES ASSISTANT MUST HAVE A BIKE FROM THEIR SHOP
      - PERHAPS NOT
        - I WAS RIGHT TO GO FOR BRAKE PADS — THEY'RE LESS EXPENSIVE AND IT'S MY FIRST BIKE
        - MAYBE HE'S GOT TWO BIKES — THE OTHER IS HIGH-PERFORMANCE AND SECRET
          - I HOPE MY BIKE IS HIGH-PERFORMANCE
  - THE SALES ASSISTANT SAID IT WAS A MULTI-SURFACE BIKE
    - MAYBE HE'S A BAD SALESMAN
    - HE SAID IT WAS THE IDEAL BIKE FOR RIDES LIKE THIS
      - MAYBE HE'S NOT TELLING THE TRUTH
      - MAYBE HE THINKS IT'S TRUE

- I'LL PUNCTURE MY INNER TUBE
  - I NEED A BIKE
  - I HAVE NO EXPERIENCE OF INNER TUBES
    - I'LL HAVE TO REPAIR MY BIKE ALL ALONE IN THE DEPTHS OF THE COUNTRYSIDE
      - MAYBE IT'S NOT JUST ABOUT MARKETING
      - MAYBE IT WON'T WORK FOR ME

- IT DOESN'T LOOK LIKE A PERFORMANCE BIKE BUT THAT'S ANOTHER REASON WHY I LIKE IT
  - MAYBE I'M BEING SOLD A BIT OF ROMANTICISM AND NOSTALGIA
  - THERE MAY BE A GOOD REASON WHY PERFORMANCE BIKES ARE UGLY

- I'LL HAVE TO FIND THINGS TO EAT
  - IF I GO TO RESTAURANTS, I'LL BE SKINT
  - IF I HAVE PICNICS IN THE COLD AND RAIN, I'LL ONLY HAVE THE ENERGY TO CRY
  - A PICNIC WILL BE TOO HEAVY

- I'LL HAVE TO VISIT MY FAMILY IN LONDON
  - THEY'LL ASK ME IF I KNOW HOW TO REPAIR A FLAT TYRE
    - DO YOU SAY 'REPAIR' FOR A FLAT TYRE?
  - THEY'LL SEE I DON'T KNOW HOW TO DO ANYTHING ON MY OWN AND THAT I DON'T EVEN KNOW HOW MY BIKE WORKS

- I'LL HAVE TO BE AT THE POINT OF DEPARTURE: LONDON
  - GOING BY TRAIN: EXPENSIVE AND TAKES AGES. I'LL BE SKINT.
  - GOING BY PLANE: IRRESPONSIBLE BUT CHEAP. WE NEED TO STOP FLYING.

- EVEN THOUGH I KNOW THE NAMES OF THE VILLAGES I'LL GO THROUGH, I NEED TO CHOOSE A ROUTE
  - PERHAPS I CAN'T RELY ON GOOGLE'S ALGORITHMS WHEN CLICKING ON THE BIKE
  - PERHAPS THE BIKEMAP ALGORITHM ISN'T ANY BETTER
  - I DO A TEST: GOOGLE, BIKEMAP AND MAPS.ME ALL SUGGEST THREE SLIGHTLY DIFFERENT ROUTES
  - I SHOULD STICK TO GREENWAYS, VELOROUTES AND EUROVELOS

- IF I GET LOST I'LL BE LOST
- I'LL BE ALONE

- SOMETIMES IT'LL RAIN AND BE SLIPPERY

- TAKE SOMETHING TO WEAR
  - TAKE FABRICS THAT DON'T SCRATCH MY SKIN
    - I'LL SWEAT
    - I'LL BE TOO HOT
    - I'LL BE TOO COLD
  - MY CLOTHES WILL HAVE TO DRY QUICKLY
    - WHICH FABRICS DRY QUICKLY?
  - I'LL HAVE TO DO SOME WASHING ON MY REST DAYS
  - I NEED TO REVIEW MY WHOLE WARDROBE

- I'LL BE LUGGING BAGS ON THE WAY THERE
  - I MUST TRAVEL LIGHT
  - I'VE NO WAY OF SELECTING THE BEST ROUTE
    - IT WILL BE DARK SOMETIMES
    - PERHAPS I SHOULD RING THE HUMANS WHO WORK IN THESE VILLAGES AND CHECK WHAT SURFACE EACH ROUTE HAS

- I'LL BE COLD AT NIGHT

- FIND ACCOMMODATION FOR LESS THAN 50 € A NIGHT
  - FIND PRETTY AND COSY B&Bs
  - B&Bs WITH VACANCIES EVERY NIGHT
  - I'LL BE UNHAPPY WRITING IN EERIE, SQUALID PLACES

- FIND A WAY TO NAVIGATE IN THE WILD
  - FIND THE BEST VILLAGES TO SEE OR IT'LL BE A TOTAL FAILURE
    - I WON'T HAVE TIME TO VISIT THEM
    - I'LL HAVE TOO MUCH TIME AND WILL GET BORED
  - FIND MY WAY WITH A PAPER MAP
    - IF IT RAINS, THE PAPER WILL TEAR
    - WITH A PAPER MAP, I'LL HAVE TO STOP TO CHECK WHERE I AM

- I'VE GOT IN MIND IDEAL LITTLE COUNTRY AUBERGES BUT CAN'T FIND THEM AS I ALWAYS END UP ON BOOKING.COM OR EBOOKERS.COM
  - I WON'T FIND PRETTY ROUTES, WILL END UP ON ROADS AND WON'T BE HAPPY BEING OVERTAKEN AT 80 KM AN HOUR

- I'LL HAVE NOWHERE TO SLEEP
- I COULD HAVE AN ACCIDENT, CYCLING FOR A MONTH

- I'LL HAVE TO CHARGE MY IPHONE EVERY NIGHT
  - MY PHONE DIES
  - SOMETIMES I'LL FORGET
  - MY IPHONE GOES WRONG
  - THE COMPASS PLAYS UP AND I GO OFF IN THE OPPOSITE DIRECTION

I've also got this little list stored somewhere inside my head but it's floating around amongst other, far less relevant items which still take up just as much room. The list is non-exhaustive, of course. If I dwell too long on one point, it swells, bursts, and gives birth to three others which, in turn, mature very quickly. In order to choose my priorities, I must be able to define these items, lay them all out in front of me, understand them, have a poke around in them. I endeavour to do a brainstorming session and create a mind-map from my mental hurricane. Then I realise that if I go down that road, there's a strong possibility I'll include my life, my death, what the hell we're all doing here, what the hell you're doing reading this, and what the hell I'm doing writing it, and then, well... I know I'm approaching a massively time-consuming trap. So, with a sort of eyelid sweep and brain swipe, I decide to temporarily deny this extensive procreation of items that are raging inside me. I try to be a bit more like the people I see, i.e. efficient, even if it means remaining on the edge.

After struggling for hours, I finally come across the official routes in formats I can upload to my Maps.me app that I plan to use for navigation. First in GPX format that I convert to KML because that's what my app understands. Not me. Even after reading on the Internet, I don't understand the difference at all. It's inconvenient and distracting. But as there are so many things in this world that are alien to me, I accept that someone else holds the key to this knowledge, and I dutifully swallow the mush of indistinct elements and stop giving a damn. It's a mini-denial.

But it's a victory as I've finally succeeded in finding my routes and bringing them up on my navigation apps. I thought – whilst imagining my ideal website – that they would be easy to find, but no. Of course, I'm a total novice and nothing about this process comes naturally to me. Once the KML files are registered on my iPhone, I open them with Maps.me and have fun zooming in and using my finger to explore the whole route by downloading complete maps that the app suggests in pop-ups. The time it takes with my finger gives me some idea of the time it's going to take on two wheels.

This little win is a whole new sensation for me and I surprise myself by pausing a really juicy series, oozing with comfort, to search for other ways to find routes. The atmosphere suddenly seems less chilly and enables me to explore further. It's as though a small door has been opened. When fear disappears and curiosity takes its place, it's crazy how much fun you can have.

2nd October

I haven't decided on my stopovers yet and anxiety is back in residence. This evening is the first time in two weeks that I've listened to music. The first time since the break-up with B2. I'm falling slightly apart. I'm in constant contact with B1. We phone and text each other every day to talk about the trip which concerns him now, too, as he's going to cycle with me for the first three days.

It's 7 p.m. and I'm getting an Ikea bag ready to do my last load of washing before my departure. Clothes stacked, heart clamped, nerves smashed, I open the door of my small flat onto the stairwell, and dinner smells and family sounds emerge from the building and envelop me, like in a cartoon strip. In the time it takes to get to the laundry room on the first floor, the smells changing with each landing lift me out of my gloom. I remember that the world is still there; other people, too, with their warmth and daily life.

My Spotify list isn't on shuffle, and it plays the soundtrack of my past few weeks. I don't know if I miss B2 a lot or not at all. He certainly isn't good for me. But listening to the music, I remember that he loved music, too. And the last time I saw him, we were at the co-working office, and he was playing a beautiful piece on the piano that I'd never heard before. An irregular shape of white lace suspended in a blue sky. When I heard him playing, I moved towards him, as though being pulled. His fingers weaving threads around my heart. I sat down next to the piano and he immediately stopped playing. He told me coldly that he was waiting for a colleague. Stunned to the core and humiliated, I went back to my workspace, feeling really stupid. So sad to lose someone who could make sounds like that.

We had talked about doing a song together. But everything was impossible between us, everything drove us to find each other and then tear each other apart. This to-ing and fro-ing was too violent for me. Everything in him was a contradiction, and everything made me want him. He had a mouth I could have watched without listening to. He talked profusely – self-fascinated monologues that often bored me senseless. He was arrogant and scathing whilst claiming to be inept and inoffensive. I never knew where I stood – was he going to be scornful or caring?

I try and remember that mouth now. I find it hard to believe that I kissed it, many times, that I had it. I had him. And I let him go. He slipped away from me. He didn't want me anymore. He never wanted me. He only wanted himself. Another version of himself through me. He didn't want to know me and didn't want me to know him. When he closed his eyes and a soft smile played on his lips, that was it. He would barricade himself in. He'd try and confuse the issue with this smile that desperately said, 'I'm fine I'm fine I'm fine.' The sealed mouth and mute eyelids implied, 'No, you can't come in here, because here we're pretending to be in harmony. And you don't know how to pretend.'

I suddenly come across a song we used to listen to. We secretly imagined that we were singing it together, ironically. We wanted to write a song together, ironically. It suited who we were. He told me once that essential lavender oil was a cure-all. 'Really?' I asked, 'It cures all problems?' and he said, 'Yes, you see that ball of fluff gathering in the corner of your room? You could put a drop on it and, poof, it'd be gone!' I liked him so much. I was drunk on him. I thought I'd found a real gem.

And now I don't know where to channel this energy of sadness, so I hug the cushions on my sofa and weep as I watch the rain beating on my windows. Life is beautiful. I feel so lucky. I savour the pure sadness. It suddenly stabs me right in the heart and I'd like to cry more. I'd like to cry everything out but something in me doesn't believe in it. My tears won't come because I tell myself I'm crying whilst watching the rain. And that just drips with the pathetic.

I imagined everything with B2. That's why he left. In fact, he never left, he just never arrived. He wasn't even here. I was always trying to clarify our positions in relation to each other, but he mystified everything. I couldn't see a thing – there was a complete fog and I lost myself in it. In such a short space of time, B2 has become a distant memory and I'm forgetting his face. But if I really concentrate, some bits fit back together and my heart leaps. His smell comes back to me. That hurts. So I try not to do it too often. I open the window and sip my herbal tea. The universe is crashing down on me tonight.

3rd October

I'm annoyed with the Maps.me app that sometimes hides names of towns from me, like Reims or Paris... Whoever approved such a system?! My sense of sadness is at its peak, and I am nothing but a humourless empty shell. The shape of B2's mouth is fading but the effect it had on me remains*. When I think of him, my organs take a beating. I can't access the feelings I've got for him. I have no influence on them, they just happen. They have a wild nature to me. If I bumped into him tomorrow, I would melt. If I bumped into him ten years from now, unless my chemical make-up changes in the meantime, the chances are I would melt then, too.

My stress, my loneliness, my fear, and my stomach constantly weigh heavily on me. I'm stressing because maybe I haven't got the most suitable pair of leggings. I'm stressing because there'll be a bar between my legs that I may not be able to throw my leg over every time I get on or off my bike. Every uncertain and unknown entity is a source of disconcerting anxiety. But everything is

---

*   This word suggests to me that it will last a lifetime, until I am nothing but remains myself.

planned as far as Reims. That's more than a third, almost half. Perhaps there'll be too many kilometres between each stopover. Perhaps there won't be enough. Perhaps there'll be too many breaks. Perhaps not enough. What will happen in Newhaven when I have to leave B1? I'm scared of being unhappy during my trip, of losing hope. Because I'll only have myself to rely on. And I don't have much faith in that. There will just be me. If I panic, the whole world will be shaken. If I'm sad, the whole world will be tainted.

4th October

In the bike equipment shop, I freeze – I've got to choose the number and type of cycling shorts to take with me. There are seven options:

- Long leggings
- Short leggings
- Short shorts
- Long, padded cycling leggings
- Short, padded cycling leggings
- Short, padded cycling shorts
- A pair of padded, cycling knicker-things

I think I'll take three items out of the seven. Three is good. There must be a perfect combination. As soon as I think of a good combination of three, the four that are left taunt me, so I go back to square one.

The knickers are transparent and serve as an undergarment. I couldn't wear them on their own. I'd have to combine them with supplementary, unpadded bottoms. The others could either be worn by themselves or with something else (according to the combinations). I could wear the short, padded shorts with the long leggings if it was cold. I could also wear the short, padded leggings on their own. Also, the long leggings could be worn for activities other than cycling once this trip is over, whereas the padded items are specifically for cycling, plus they cost more.

After two hours in the shop, I'm offered a cup of coffee even though I'm in deep phone conversation with Noah, my English bike salesman, who tells me the colour I ordered will be ready a day later than expected, that is the 10th of October. Would I like to choose a different colour that will be available in time? Or would I prefer to wait an extra day for the chosen colour? I refuse the coffee with a vague gesture. Can't he see I'm pacing up and down? I make my way around the shop in fits and starts, with neither coat nor bag, which are on the table with a scribbled list. Occasionally, I step over some accessories for sale that obstruct my path. I'll ring the Englishman back later. I feel my mad hair is betraying me with its wild, screeching appearance. I'm in a state of maximum perspiration. I sit down near the table where my things are. I get my breath back after my ramblings and am suddenly imbued with hope in humanity, so I beat my way through the crowd of items on display towards the young member of staff, the one who wanted me to have a coffee. I would like him to help me. Drastically help me.

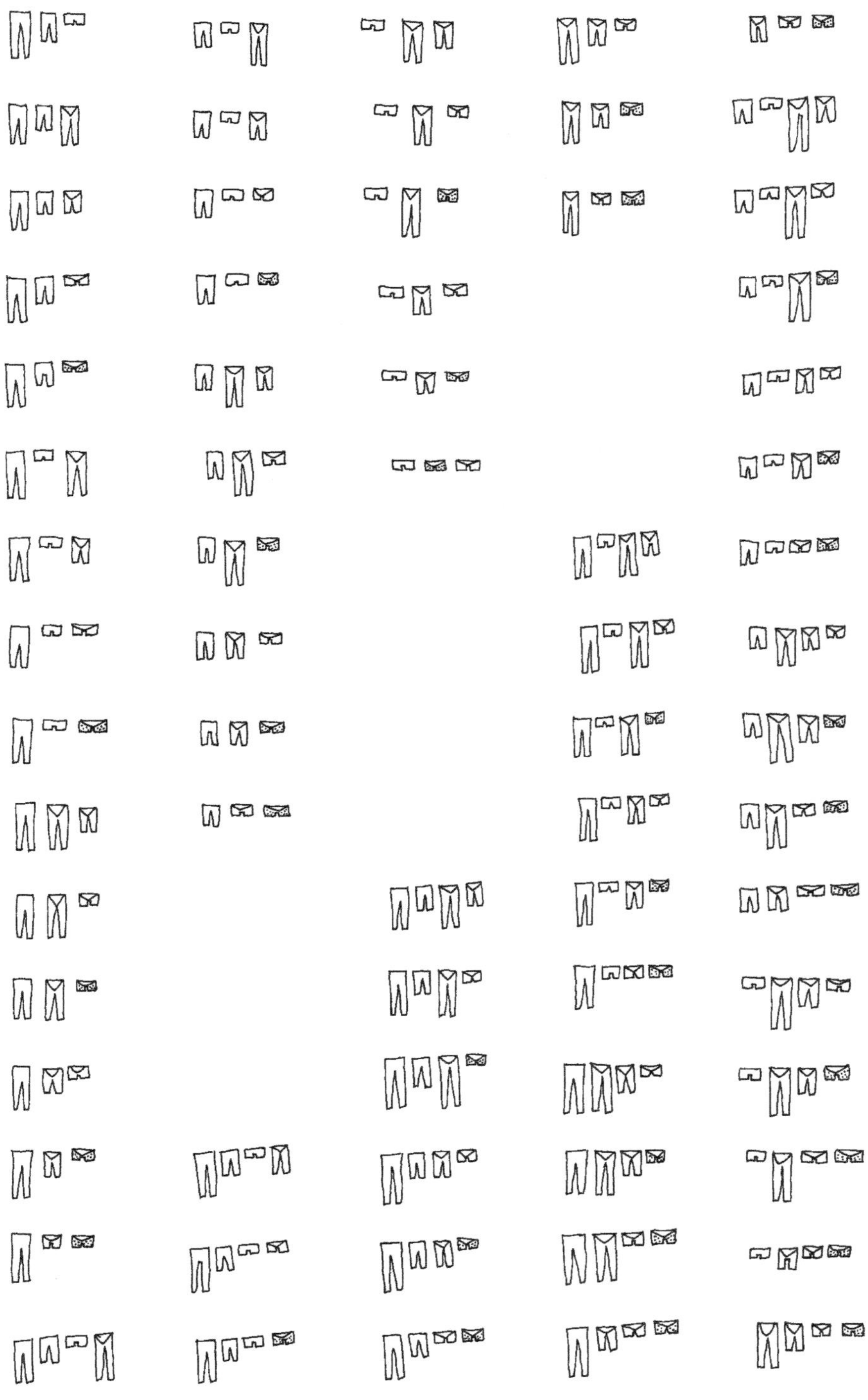

I need him to understand my temporary state of derangement and reassure me with his expert opinion. Unfortunately, he just pretends. He doesn't listen to me. He talks too much and about pointless things. He interrupts me to say, 'It's good to be warm when it's cold.' Eventually, I opt for the combination of short, padded cycling shorts; short, padded cycling leggings; and long leggings.

In the afternoon, I find some Gore-Tex trainers that are supposed to be rainproof. Yet again, I'm at the mercy of incompetent, pseudo professionals who couldn't care less. 'I'm also looking for a head torch I can put on a bike helmet that isn't flat at the front. What would you recommend?' The sales assistant looks about twelve to me. She escorts me to the lamps I'd already located, and we read out the labels together, in chorus. 'So, we've got that... Or there's this one here, as well...' she says, pointing to them. I've got a choice between Visual Assault number 1: some sort of *Frozen* thing; and Visual Assault number 2: hunting and fishing 2050. I look up, my eyes aching. 'Isn't there anything else?' She reluctantly has a rummage around and I find a black head torch that seems far less offensive. At this point in our exchange, I would like to do an about-turn and head for the till as any contribution from her won't improve my ability to choose a light. But, out of compassion for her young age, I ask, 'Is this one OK?' She retorts, 'Now, that's more expensive.' Sure enough, after performing a quick calculation, I arrive at the same conclusion as her: one of the numbers is bigger. And it is indeed the item I'm enquiring about: 59.90 Swiss francs, double the price of *Frozen*. Didn't she have any intention of showing me this lamp? On what basis? At no point had I told her my budget, nor given any hint of my financial situation. I do a quick mental scan of the clothes I'm wearing and the state of me today. I forgive her this slight professional slip but am prepared to pay that price to shut her baby beak once and for all. 'Yes, I'll take that one,' I say. She recites from the label. 'So, that one lights up to 20 metres away, or there's this one that lights up to 40 metres.' I've never cycled using a head torch, so I don't know how far I need to see ahead in relation to my average speed, which I also don't know. 'I don't know how far I need to see ahead in relation to my speed,' I tell her, 'but I'll take the one for twenty…' She interrupts me with the excitement of a child who knows the answer, and cries, 'Twenty metres is about as far as the wall over there,' pointing to the wall 3 metres away. I turn to look at her, and my face is probably glowing with satisfaction and the suppressed desire to scoff, then I see that she's embarrassed, realising her error of judgment. Her cheeks go bright red, so I thank her and go to the till. I could have crushed her. How kind of me not to.

5th October

6th October

MY RECTANGLE OF BELONGINGS

7th October

I didn't even realise I'd forgotten to write anything. Not realising you've forgotten is the same as forgetting... After scrunching up my brain for a moment with that thought, I finish the housework in my flat. All my belongings are arranged on the floor in a rectangle which I find satisfying:

- a stick of solid deodorant
- solid shampoo
- solid toothpaste
- solid soap
- contact lens solution with case
- a spare pair of monthly-disposable lenses
- my house keys on an earplug-carrying keyring
- a tube of cream for sports injuries
- hand sanitiser gel
- disinfectant
- essential lavender oil
- cleaning wipes
- arnica granules
- some Compeed
- a tiny tube of healing gel

- plasters of all shapes and sizes
- tissues
- a bag for aforementioned first-aid products
- my turquoise notebook with elastic band
- my handlebar-bag-occasional-bag-handbag
- a phone charger
- my British passport
- my purse with my Swiss identity card
- lip balm
- headphones
- a lighter
- a bag of tampons
- a comb
- my prescription specs and their cloth-case-combo
- my sunglasses
- a Swiss Army knife
- a phone holder for a bike
- another one with a touch-sensitive case for wet weather
- two reflective strips for my arms and legs
- the head torch
- my helmet
- my phone charger
- four pairs of knickers
- two ballpoint pens
- a swimming costume
- my printed plane ticket
- a book
- a travel towel in a bag
- a padded coat in a bag

- Gore-Tex cycling gloves
- an emerald-green, cashmere woolly hat
- a waterproof cover for my belongings
- a pair of ski socks
- two pairs of sports socks
- a knee-high pair
- my brother's blue merino top
- a petrol-blue, sports material T-shirt
- a black cotton vest-top
- a cashmere neckband
- a red-and-navy striped cotton T-shirt
- my Gore-Tex, Klein-blue cagoule
- a midnight-blue and coral-pink fluorescent fleece
- a steel-grey cashmere jumper
- a black merino jumper with a zipped collar
- grey cotton jogging bottoms
- my long leggings
- water-resistant trousers
- my short, padded cycling shorts
- my short, padded cycling leggings
- a pair of jeans
- Gore-Tex trainers
- and my two cycle bags for the luggage rack

What a lot of work to get to this point! I think calm finally reigns. It feels like everything is coming to a beginning. I'm glad the unbearable treading of water is over at last.

8th October

I escape from my flat with the two cycle bags hanging off the ends of my arms. Blood starts flowing through my veins again as my leg muscles finally come back to life, and my lungs refill with air. I've packed about 7 kilos. And then I've got the bag I'll hook over the handlebars. I'm not comfortable with pretty little handbags, so I always try and get by with rucksacks or bags with a specific purpose, like for carrying a camera. That way, form follows function and you know why you've got a bag like that. I struggle with things that have a random shape (except in certain cases where it manages to speak to me). In this instance, my two bags are entirely and specifically designed to be attached to the luggage rack. In fact, no ergonomics have been considered for carrying them manually. Inevitably, after five minutes' walk to the *métro*, my little trainee biceps are rather appalled that I'm inflicting such unfamiliar exertion on them. They'll get their own back tomorrow.

The train is there, so I propel myself forward and my arms and bags follow suit. The doors only just manage to close behind me. With my bags on the floor, I unfurl my fingers and slowly stand up. My hands and cheeks are the same breathless shade of red. I haven't even raised my head to analyse the human landscape of this *métro* carriage – they're still just indistinct forms – when I hear a 'So, you're off?' directed at me. I turn round and see Jo, a cyclist I wrote to yesterday to tell her I was going. I know she used to be a bike courier and has won several competitions. I'm thrilled to see her and take it as a good sign.

9th October

London.
I went under this Ladbroke Grove bridge with my cousin and his guitar last night when I arrived. There are loads of people around today. Although my eyes are clouded, I still recognise the familiar, oblong shape of B1, standing there waiting for me*. At this moment, my happiness is complete and absolute – there's not a shred of darkness. I jump for joy at seeing him. His face betrays a similar excitement, but it's controlled beneath a layer of reason and realism. If I had turned up looking depressed, I think he would've taken on the opposite role and sparkled in my place. He is a balancing agent. I feel at home with him.

We go and eat in Portobello, then join the Extinction Rebellion demonstration up to Buckingham Palace, Westminster, and Trafalgar Square. There are craft stalls, food stalls, and groups of people are making costumes for the march, whilst others are in a circle, singing improvised harmonies. The atmosphere is sizzling. Borders come crashing down. We're all simultaneously

---

* And here you meet B1. He's the only B you will meet. The other will remain hidden in the shadows of my mind. He will never emerge.

buzzing with life and simply having this in common allows us to float from one group to another, whereas in normal times we would be anonymous strangers.

We glide down towards Shepherd's Bush, then go to the cinema. In the evening, we put a mattress in B1's bedroom for me. During the night, I'm cold in the sleeping bag that seems to be made entirely of labels, Velcro and zips. I can hear them in the darkness, conspiring against my sleep the day before the big departure, and I'm fractiously frustrated with them.

10th October

It would seem that I was plunged into a long, deep slumber whilst I lived the craziest and most intense relationship of my life with B2 and it's now time to wake up. It's not too much of a shock, since everything looks the same as it did when I fell asleep: B1 is there and is attentive. But there's still the bitter taste of unwelcome dreams, strewn like rubbish, that linger throughout the morning.

When I ring the cycle shop, I learn that I can't collect my bike until early afternoon. I had planned to get there about 9.30, so our schedule is thrown out. As I've already had to cancel my first night's accommodation in Crawley, north London, because the colour I wanted wasn't available for the 9th of October, I'm itching to get going. Today's itinerary consists of taking the train to East Grinstead (not far from Crawley) to make up for a day's delay, then to ride as far as Rotherfield where we'll spend the night: just 25 kilometres and an hour and a half of cycling, according to Google Maps, for our first day. All websites recommend starting with short stages, to gradually get into the swing of things. In this case, the short stretch will mean we don't have to ride at night.

After a plentiful and bland brunch in a tiny restaurant filled with gossiping cops, we head towards Shoreditch. With my bags still hanging off the ends of my arms, we turn into Brick Lane. In this branch of the original Bristol workshop, I finally meet my bicycle. The object that will become an extension of my limbs and enhancement of my muscles over the next three weeks. It's gorgeous. Petrol blue. Medium-sized Reynolds 520 steel frame, 27 gears, Shimano levers on the ends of the handlebars, Brooks brown leather saddle, luggage rack, mud guards, brake shoes, two bottle holders, Schwalbe Delta Cruiser 28-millimetre tyres – and the whole lot weighs 10.9 kilos. Everything essential and nothing superfluous. I've also got a small pair of lamps with elastic attachments. I finally fit my cycle bags to the back of the bike. They're bursting with impatience and their little clips immediately snap into place as they bite the luggage rack.

When we leave the shop, the adventure begins… on the left! This new sensation, perched on my metal frame, is pretty unsettling, like being driven at 100 kilometres an hour lying on the windscreen. The London air blows past me, whipping my cheeks.

East Grinstead.
As we get off the train, I open the app with the route that will lead us to our beds. The sun is already low in the sky. It smells of autumn and the north. We pedal along a lengthy wooded track that's suspended in time and peppered with small, red-brick bridges. Then we join a path that runs between raindrops, fields, and forests. It

is dotted with cottages (still in red brick) that are both creepy and comforting at the same time. Spooky and welcoming. But I know that, inside, people are sipping their tea and nibbling on biscuits. The afternoon fades, pretending it's evening. Corridor-like paths weave their way around the hedges. It's now pitch black, and all of our lights (head torches and bike lamps) are switched on so we can see the route ahead. We reach what appears to be a dense forest (but which probably resembles a puny little wood in the daytime). We're going uphill, it's chucking it down, B1's saddle is soaked, and his gears keep slipping. I can hear his frustration from my bike, which seems to be guided by some external force as it's gliding along so well.

We come to a hamlet at the edge of the wood where locals have decorated each side of the road with Guy Fawkes dolls and hung life-size fabric crows from trees, probably in anticipation of Bonfire Night. By day, the display would scream collective creativity but, at this precise moment, we're extremely glad there are two of us! B1 tries to invoke various horror films but, between breaths, I sling a 'Shut it!' in his direction. I promise myself I won't let the next few days' cycling drag out so late.

Rotherfield.
We arrive far later than expected and our host doesn't seem that enamoured with our demeanour of intrepid travellers. We go inside, dripping with muddy water, apologise and, after sweetening her up a bit, climb the stairs to our room. We don't see her again all evening. Beige carpet covers the entire first floor. From the

threshold of our room, several carpeted paths go off in a more or less straight line towards little doors with wrought-iron latches. The passageways creep over different levels that are linked by mini-staircases of two or three steps. I learn the way to the bathroom. We eat in the kitchen on the ground floor, kept company by a radio that spews out sensational gunk and songs from the 1990s. I've no idea where our host has gone but, feeling sure she isn't far away, I dare not turn off the ear-splitting radio. *Nothing Compares 2 U* comes on. My eyes begin to burn, my throat drops a notch, and the centre of my body contracts. As much as it annoys me, I'm not immune to clichés. B1 tucks into his stir-fried noodles with vegetables and, bringing the fork to his mouth, asks me what I thought of my first day. I slowly begin to sob into my bowl of noodles that don't require any added salt. I wonder if I have the right to cry in front of a bloke that isn't mine. During my time with B2, I hardly cried at all. Something didn't allow it.

B1 is on the bed, looking at his phone. I'm lying face-down on the carpet, writing in my notebook. When I was little and complained of stomach-ache at the table, I was told to lie down on the floor, on my front. A groundhug. Your organs are reassured and feel less alone. At times, my energy slips away for a while, and I lie my head next to my turquoise book. I try and make myself understand that this trip is really here! It's here now. With my ear buried amongst British dust mites, I can hear, in one of the many rooms I haven't seen, that our host is glued to a detective series.

– Peter, she's gone.
– I know, but... What if...
– ...
– Richard, the door! There's something behind the door!
– Good God, was it there all this time?
– I don't know. We need to speak to both father and son and find out exactly what they saw and when.
– I'll leave that up to you, Lorraine.
– Good night, Gareth.
– Night, Richard.
– C'mon, Lorraine.

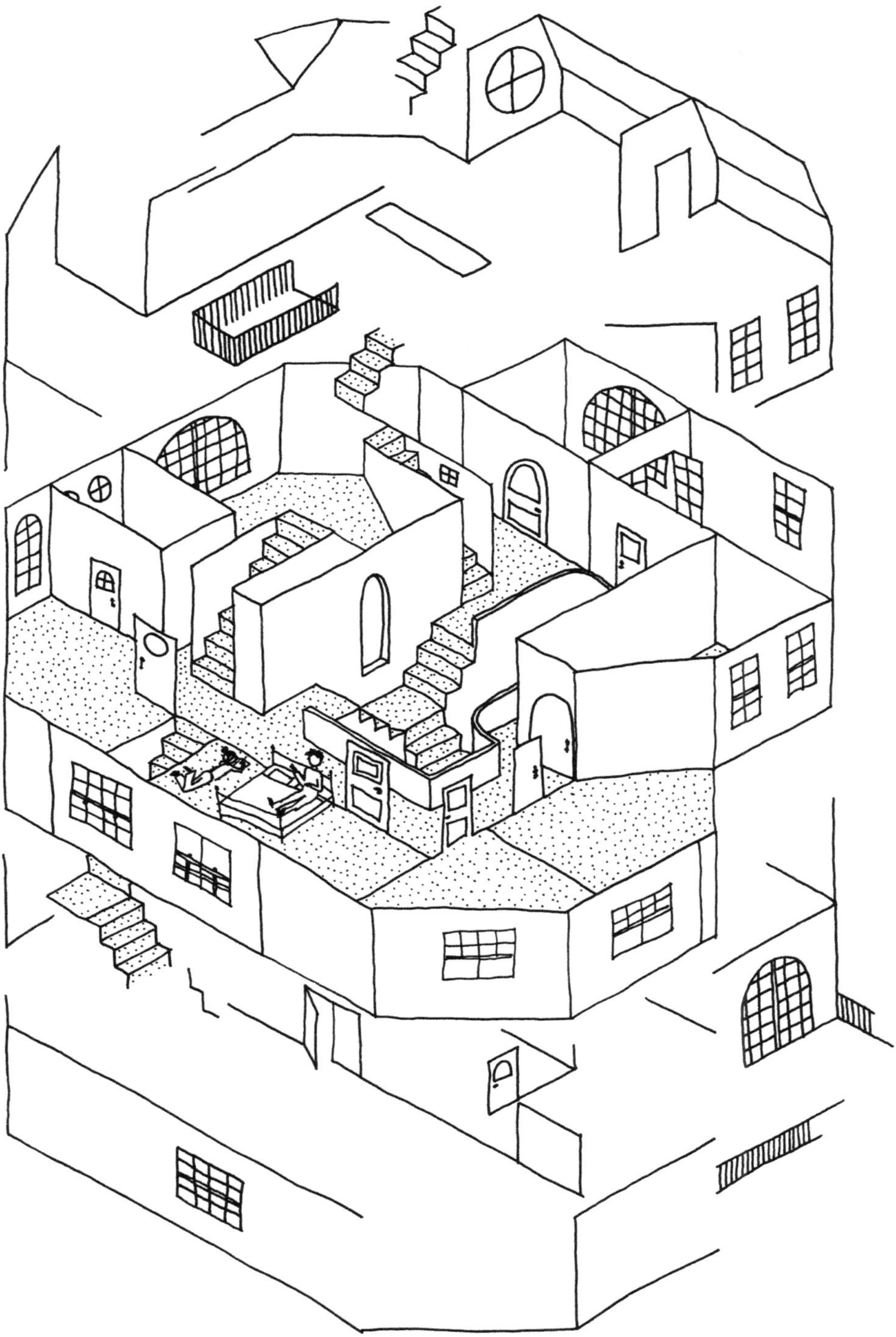

11th October

It's drizzling and there's high cloud. Sometimes the sun pokes through, then disappears under its duvet again without actually going to bed. As I pedal, the thought comes to me that everything is perfect right now. 'This bike is the worst bloody thing in the world,' yells B1, who is absolutely fuming. The poor man has borrowed an old, rusty mountain bike affair with huge suspension springs and a soaked sponge for a saddle from yesterday's rain. Its small wheels and wide tyres give it the look of a motorbike. As we're going uphill in a forest to get to a main route, I can hear his gears slipping again. B1 stops in a fit of rage, lets go of his bike that falls into the grass, and threatens to leave it behind if it doesn't behave. I focus on the climb. When I get to the top, I lean my bike against a tree and take a few swigs of water which is infused with plastic from the cheap bottle that came free with the bicycle. B1 arrives on foot, dragging his bike, livid. He holds out a cable to me that was for his front brake.

As we approach Litlington, the terrain flattens out and the ground is waterlogged. Up to this point, we've been riding in straight, hedge-lined corridors. Now, the scenery opens up and we can see the horizon in the distance. Patches of sea start to sneak in on either side of the landscape. All the shapes are misty. Long and flat. And in a shade of blue or green. Then, just past a little knoll, when we're at right angles to the seashore, the wind begins to scream in our faces for no reason as the view is nothing to write home about. The clouds take up all the room and a lack of shadows prevents any contrast. In any case, there's nothing to see: small, yellow-foamed waves on the left which are making far more noise than necessary, and a retirement home on the right replicated until the road goes out of sight.

Newhaven.
B1 is really annoying me with his constant complaining, and I secretly remember why we're no longer together. On several occasions, we bicker a bit like we did in the past. We hurl criticisms at each other that are only permitted between couples, and I suddenly have to stop myself from running my hand through his hair or stroking his neck. We talk about it, laughing, and he tells me he suffers from the same brain malfunction. I feel a profound love for him and his presence comforts and completes me. We go to sleep in the same bed and, as I'm dropping off, I remain very much aware of the platonic boundary in the middle of the mattress. That night, I have dreams of turf war. I know that tomorrow will be a totally different story.

12th October

When I wake up, I realise I've taken all the covers and that poor B1 is curled up under a triangle-shaped margin* of sheet. We're both very far apart, despite the small bed. He swears he isn't cold and didn't even notice.

With B2, I would sit up in bed to assess the amount of room we both had. He was permanently spread out over 75% of the surface and that irritated me because I don't like to sleep pressed up against someone**. If he was awake, I'd ask him to move over and he'd lie on his side, right on the edge of the bed so he didn't take up more than 10 centimetres of space and could play the victim. If he was asleep, I would whisper to him to move and gently encourage him with my hand on his shoulder. But this was far less effective as he would just turn his head and maybe retract an arm. So I found myself pushing

---

*   Section of duvet cover with no filling inside because it's poorly distributed, or the cover is the wrong size. A sheet margin can be very inconvenient in bed as the weight is uneven on the body and the thin material often falls on airways and obstructs them, whereas the part with filling has a much better hold. Heavy and light at the same time.

** It's the prolonged contact with skin that irks me. In fact, even when I'm alone in bed, I make sure the duvet or pillows keep the maximum number of limbs apart.

him as hard as I could. He had a flawless way of sleeping. He'd go right through the night without moving a muscle or making the slightest sound. Except when he was sleep-walking. Once, in the middle of the night, he suddenly sat up in bed and declared that I must not move on any account, that I was perfectly placed in the centre of the drawing! Apart from these rare episodes, his sleep was smooth and impenetrable, just like his remarkably polished and pore-free skin. Perhaps it was thanks to these reptilian features that he could slither, hide in recesses (of my mind), and escape with a flick of his tail.

After breakfast, we go to Newhaven port. My heart is heavy. A dead weight, even. It's time for an umpteenth break-up. B1 waits with me in the long queue of vehicles. Just before the ticket booth, we hug each other between two cars. I sob as I have never sobbed before. He holds me up. His eyes are moist, but firm. I can feel the windscreens' silent looks. My passport is ready (to pass through the port), and so is my ticket. They scan it at the booth without saying a word, and I move forward in the queue. Distancing myself further from B1 to join another queue, various organs seem to rip deep inside me. I've got hiccups and I'm producing fat, fleshy tears at an alarming rate. An enormous woman in a hi-viz orange vest, in charge of passenger control, waves me through to the left. 'You all right, love?' I'm in a daze and reply with a curled-up 'Yeah' that veers towards the high notes, then peters out. I'm asked if I've got a knife in my bag and I answer whilst wiping my sopping wet mush that, yes, I've got a Swiss Army knife. Each time I turn round to look at him, B1 smiles at me encouragingly.

ORGANS STAGE A WALK-OUT

People can see me and that's too bad for them. My cheeks can no longer tell the difference between the drops falling from the sky and those from my eyes. Everything merges together and I'm suddenly part of a much larger world.

You're allowed to walk around crying here as it's a place of separation. I feel a sense of legitimacy or even dignity – I'm the only human amongst all the machines with their metal shells, and I'm in direct communication with the wind. I slowly continue my way along Lane 3, in this half-motorway, half-abattoir place, and have to keep stopping every 2 metres. A man in hi-viz motions to me to get on my bike. I swiftly do as I'm told then immediately have to put my feet back on the ground as the queue isn't going anywhere. I question the reasoning behind that instruction. Then I climb onto the iron footbridge that connects the boat with terra firma. It seems oversized and is studded with metal cylinders about 3 centimetres high that surely won't do my tyres any good. Someone gestures vaguely to me that I should head for the end of the huge hangar. Several vehicles are already parked up but there's not a human being in sight. I'm on the edge of the world, between borders where only the crossing staff dare venture, where only they know the codes. I look for signage. I see some notices displaying completely random numbers and symbols. I wonder if the smooth-running of the ferry depends on these incomprehensible markings.

Once inside, I find a place at the back of the boat (I think) and sit down to prepare my nest for the next four hours. My face is still puffy, but the acute pain of being torn apart has dulled. I receive a message from B1. It's a photo of me going through check-in. My back is turned to the camera and my shoulders are raised a bit too high. From the front, you'd have seen my disintegration at that moment. The boat suddenly starts to move. It shakes. So does my hand as I write. Outside, the gigantic footbridge is drawn up and stowed in the ferry. That's it, I'm at sea. Looking online, I discover that the French name for the English Channel, *La Manche*, refers to its elongated shape that looks like a sleeve... I'm not blown away by this analogy and wonder why, of all things, this particular object was chosen. *Phallus Britannique* (or *Français*, depending on your point of view... and on the size) would've had more of an impact. But rather off-putting. While writing, I can't think of anything else elongated (is that worrying?), so I look up and notice celebratory noise around me. Not many people on board at first glance, but some teenagers are using the crossing as an excuse for a party on the floor above. Some people are playing cards, others are reading the paper, but the majority are on their phones.

    I divide an A4 sheet into sections and draw up a calendar of the next few days, in an attempt to better understand my trip by visualising it. I'd like to be able to follow and respect the shape of my brain. I'm exhausted. Maybe because of those first kilometres. Maybe because there's nowhere to go today. Or maybe it's emotional exhaustion. I'd like to untangle the Bs. Understand what's happening to me. I wonder how much this ferry is polluting the waters. I struggle to keep my thoughts on track as I write. I think about B2 again and it's as though he'd never existed, as though I'd invented him. Our relationship was entirely imagined by me, from start to finish. Hence its impossibility. No-one wants to be in a relationship with themselves. Apart from B2, perhaps...

They announce our arrival in Dieppe, so I put away my turquoise notebook and other belongings. I'm thirsty but can't bring myself to drink my plastic water. I buy a bottle of water that tastes plastic-free (but is contained in PET, nonetheless) and I accidentally thank the French waiter in English just because he's pale and podgy.

Dieppe.
Arriving in the port defies all human scale. The liner docks thanks to a yellow Playmobil toy that heaves it in with blue string and positions it alongside buoys the size of silos, like giant Tic-Tacs adorned with tiny lorry tyres. Waves that make it as far as the coast are smashed against concrete 'X's, thrown there as if by accident, and melting into the water, like an abandoned game of jacks.

I go down to get my bike, unlock it, and set off on a kind of mini-motorway: no pedestrians, a 50-centimetre strip of grass along the edge, neatly placed between the tarmac and the Channel-side wire fencing. The French name for this strip of sea could just as well have been the 'Margin' as the 'Sleeve'. Now *there's* something elongated, I think to myself.

To reach where Valentine and her other half (whose name I can't remember) live, I've got to wind my way round and climb a small hill to the east of the town centre. As my bike is brilliant, it's easy. On the advert for the accommodation, all photos of the living room are taken from practically identical angles and the television is the focal point of each one. It's switched on, of course, and there's a different programme in every photo.

When I arrive, the bloke whose name I can't remember is very enthusiastic. As he greets me, he's closely followed by two microscopic dogs (probably Japanese inventions) that chirp at me. I wonder how I know they're dogs. Probably a process of elimination. As they don't resemble anything else. They're quite jittery and are both called Lola. One belongs to them and the other to Valentine's mother. I wonder who named their dog second.

Inside the house, there's an explosion of grey, lilac, sky blue, and red. Every object screams its decorative function, and most of them sparkle. A mirrored lamp, candles that look like cupcakes, pink and white wooden hearts hanging in gold and silver frames. But there's also a metal 'Route 66' sign and canvases printed with extravagant illustrations, saturated with colours of urban scenes. They haven't dared let the object simply be what it is, naked. They felt they had to add an extra layer of affectation. 'Valentine did all the interior design!' proudly proclaims the chap whose name escapes me. 'Ah,' I say, with the intention of a smile. I inevitably form an idea of the kind of person she is from these fripperies. When I go into the living room, the television is obviously on and the micro-dogs each position themselves on a sofa, as though charging their batteries. There are shiny, muscle-bound people on the TV screen. 'It's *The Battle of the Couples*,' says the nameless man. Have I heard of it? No, I haven't.

He tells me about their other guest, 'a Russian student who keeps herself to herself,' he says. Moments later, she emerges from her room, and we introduce ourselves. Her introversion is almost a discipline. I shake her hand and feel just a slight breeze in mine. An awkwardness descends upon us, and she mumbles that she's going out for dinner. No-Name gives her a few recommendations in French, but she doesn't acknowledge them. It's so uncomfortable that I have to stop myself from speaking on her behalf. I take refuge in my room.

A few hours later, when I'm sitting bare-chested on my bed, slathering myself in *Perskindol* gel, there's a knock on my door. 'Just a minute!' I shout, putting my T-shirt back on in a panic. I open the door, and the young Russian woman is standing there with an opened cardboard box containing two little cakes. She tells me it's her birthday and that one of the cakes is for me. I'm touched and suggest we eat our cakes together in the living room. She replies, 'Oh yes, that would be nice,' like a female character from an early twentieth century novel written by a man. I suspect that's what she wanted to ask me but didn't dare. We eat our cakes whilst conversing shyly.

Her name is Marie, or *Маша* (pronounced Masha) in Russian. She hates being called Maria. She's like youth incarnate to me. Her features are delicate and smooth. She has perfect, radiant skin. Her teeth are like translucent porcelain, and her hands are adorned with impeccable nails. Her movements are dainty, like a ballerina's. I feel that she is in absolute and tight control.

Her imperfect English has a disturbing effect on my own. I falter more than her and I have trouble finding my words in French, too. My brain is synchronised with hers to enable a connection. I think the same way she does. But everything I say and do is unrefined compared with her natural grace. She's twenty today and is interested in everything, especially European culture. She tells me she comes from a village not far from Moscow, a fourteen-hour train ride away. I look at her and smile. What she likes here is the difference in scale. Everything is so close yet so quickly unfamiliar. She admits that she doesn't know what she wants to do in life, and her cheeks descend to a deeper pink. I tell her that she's lucky not to know as it implies having a choice, that I didn't know either when I was twenty and, quite frankly, I still haven't got a clue. She bursts out laughing. But it wasn't a joke. Despite her holding herself tightly in a compact oval shape, the atmosphere around us loses some of its tension. She says she's worried that time is running out for her and that, at nineteen, she went out and bought herself some anti-wrinkle cream. I make a 'pff' sound to gently mock this contradiction, but her fear of time actually saddens me. I point out that she's being quite hard – she demands to know herself inside-out already and, at the same time, doesn't want to accrue any signs of age, which she'd need in order to know herself. She asks me questions about my trip as it seems to interest her. She takes me very seriously and whispers that she's really looking forward to my book being published. Crazy girl.

Suddenly, the front door is barged open, and the masters of the house appear, chasing away the particles that had settled around us. 'Naomi! Maria!' cries No-Name, thrilled to see us together. In a stagnant lull, I announce that it's Maura's twentieth birthday. She delicately confirms the fact. No-Name asks us what on Earth we're doing, sitting in silence on such an occasion, and exclaims that the television should be turned on immediately to celebrate! Maura and I politely stay put, but our escape is already planned. He suggests a few shots of tequila and Maura uses this transition to say she's going to phone her parents. And I go to bed.

13th October

It's my first day of riding solo. I film myself with one arm, saying mundane things about the scenery that no-one will hear because of the wind. I'm ecstatic. On the road, I'm neither hungry nor thirsty, but I stop at a café in Le Tréport, just for the sake of it. It's a coastal town beside *La Manche* where each post in the port is topped with a seagull. When I park my bike, I grapple with my padlock and a lamppost. The lock is still rigid and distant with me. It's worse than a lack of leniency, it's downright stubborn. I tell myself it must therefore be very reliable. I'm going to have to sweet-talk it and understand its make-up.

Today's journey is fantastic. The landscape is gravitating towards the cold season and the colours are warming up. It's not cold. I've got a mission, a route in mind, and for the first time, the impression that I'm out in the world. I wind my way between fields, little nondescript towns, and the seaside.

As I approach Cayeux-sur-Mer, I can see black shapes moving on the beach. Their hammock-like form makes me think of birds, but their movements are out of proportion. I squint and see that they're actually seals!

Saint-Valéry-sur-Somme.

On arrival, I decide to have an orange and cinnamon tea because it's wet outside and my host hasn't replied for two hours. It's quite pleasant, there's no-one in this *restaurant-fromagerie* on the main street (the main street to me, anyway, as I haven't seen anywhere else). Just across the road is my accommodation for the night. The orange and cinnamon tea is too weak and far less comforting than expected.

When I'm finally united with my bed 3 metres from the cheese café, I'm confronted once again with decor of the most bewildering kind. It's as if people are afraid of not setting a decorative theme. Here, every room has one. It's Plastic Pastel Party in the living room. Every object adheres to this theme and the requisite colour code. In this case, pale pink and baby blue, apart from the black modem which blinks wildly. I feel a rush of love for it. The toilet is Yoga in the Woods. A picture of a birch tree. Dusty plastic stems shoot up from a slim vase. On the wall to the left of the loo, where I'm sitting, there are three identical canvases positioned one beneath the other. It's a photo of a branch, surrounded by other branches. With my head in my hands and elbows on my knees, I imagine my host in the interior design shop deciding to buy three of the same canvas:

1. They go well together – no style clashes;
2. The wall is fairly high and needs to be covered;
3. You can't have too much of a good thing.

I can't think of any other rational grounds for it. In my bedroom, the theme is... unclear... The four walls are covered with three different types of wallpaper, all of them black and silver. The first is embossed with haphazard vertical lines, the second is covered with enormous pseudo-baroque decorative elements, and the third is printed with framed portraits of different breeds of dog, all dressed like Napoleon, Sherlock Holmes, or Louis the Fourteenth. Some Sherlocks are wearing bicorne hats and some Louis figures are smoking a pipe. The floor-length, bulging curtains are made from a copper-coloured crepey fabric and encase the windows. They look like giant swathes of molten rock. On the very short bed, there's a deluge of gold, silver and black velvet, displayed via the medium of cushion art – thirteen in total. The whole lot gives me a feeling of seasickness. Probably also due to the extremely uneven floorboards which make everything lurch. I leave the room fairly swiftly to go and have dinner.

    I push open the door of my cheese café, say hello to the waiter, and sit in my usual spot. I'm glad to find a modicum of familiarity. Other human beings are present, putting the world to rights and lifting huge, shiny orbs of wine to their oenophile lips, with no accompanying food. I order a selection of cheeses on a slate. They're displayed in a spiral, and as I savour them in the recommended tasting order, a loud-speaker blasts songs in my ear that are as pointless as a sprinkling of sugar on a *Sugus* sweet. Loneliness burns right through me. I'm in constant contact with B1. Perhaps to feel I still exist, that I haven't been swallowed up by my own trip. I'm shattered.

14th October

Here I am on my own for the second day. The fourth day since I began the trip. When I wake up at 7.10 a.m., it's pitch black. I'm quite surprised. It's been a long while since I rubbed shoulders with this time of day. As soon as I leave my bedroom to go and brush my teeth, my host rushes to switch on the television and boil the kettle. While I'm eating my breakfast, a channel with a graffiti-tag logo fires out jerky clips in such a fast-paced montage that I can almost see the flashing lights of a cop car if I squint. I endure about five clips, which more or less all paint a picture of a woman denying a man something or a woman angry with a man who has presumably behaved badly. The situation isn't entirely clear but, at the end of the song, the singer and her friends use a hammer to smash up an old, corded telephone with a dial. Whilst all this is going on, my host chatters away at me and I make out I'm listening. The song lyrics have taken my brain hostage and I slip into passive mode. '*Oh, oh, tu préfères faire ton numéro, oh, oh.*' The dancing friends are now in a car park, flitting around the place, still looking pretty angry.

    My host complains that the rain is 'a pain in the arse'. It prevents her from doing everyday stuff, like household chores, she says. I realise from her awkward facial expressions and her meteorological misery that, last night, as I was impatiently waiting to check in to my accommodation, my host was very much at home, saw my calls and messages, but hadn't finished her 'bloody housework'. Her agitation and language give her away. She feigns surprise when I reply that, yes, her Wi-Fi is really good. I manage to escape about 8.15 a.m. after a nauseating breakfast. My appetite is always out of sorts in the morning.

It's not quite daylight yet, or perhaps it's due to the clouds. My saddle is soaked as I had to leave my bike outside all night. But it's OK, I'm wrapped up in my waterproof gear. The jacket and trousers. Protected from everything. The route is long, flat, and beautiful. I move away from the sea and follow the Canal de la Somme on the V30 greenway, going towards Amiens. I've been waiting for this moment for several weeks and yet I'm a bit deflated. There's gravel on the ground which, on a bike like mine, is equivalent to walking barefoot in sand. At first glance, it's nice and romantic but, in reality, you can't make any progress and it sticks to everything. The scenery is breath-taking. The trees are turning yellow, and the temperature is mild. A river runs against me, heading for the sea. The wind follows it. Perhaps it's because of them that I feel a bit neglected. I come across a lot of ducks having a nap on the grass verges. I try to slip by quietly, so I don't make them jump, but often a mother duck lifts her head, quacks a 'What?' at me in Duck, then, seeing I'm already a long way off, stuffs her head back in her feathers. There are hardly any human beings. I don't meet a single one going in the same direction as me, let alone on a bike. As I go past the chateau and its gardens in Long, I notice a walker chatting on her own beside the canal. Something about the weather, I believe.

Then, as I go past this woman, I spot her conversational partner on the other side of the canal, complaining about the headaches this wind is giving her. They're discussing trivial things 30 metres apart, like people on neighbouring balconies. At times, the canal is so straight that I'm surprised to find I'm getting impatient. I want a challenge. I need twists and turns, signposts to disappear, my path to be flooded, my phone to die...

I stop for a picnic at the water's edge, and I use the time to read my book about dismantling the Internet. I relish and analyse every word. The writer is from *Suisse Romande*, the French-speaking part of Switzerland, and she's of the same generation as me. Her writing is impeccable and well-structured, almost scholarly. Very Swiss. I savour my little red fruits tartlet, especially the *crème pâtissière*. I'd like to eat a whole bowl of it sometime. Perhaps after my next break-up.

I think about B1. I imagine he's in Switzerland by now and that he'll soon be staying in my flat. As I'm away, I'm letting him stay there so he can take care of family matters and look for a place of his own. When I think about B1, my heart melts and turns to water, which soothes me. When I think of B2, my heart bursts into flames and becomes a fire that consumes me. I've gone from one extreme to the other. B2 never gave me anything. He would ask in frustration what more I wanted apart from his time. What a sad question. It lacks everything. As if we were providing a service to one another. He skipped over sharing and had no truck with love. In truth, he just wasn't capable of it. Like not knowing how to quench one's thirst. He showed no real interest in me but was overflowing with attention for others. During our first conversation, when we'd only exchanged a few 'Hi, how are yous', he thought it would do me good to go and chat with the other co-workers, as well. What a strange suggestion. So intrusive already. I was talking to him, wasn't that enough? The more important he became to me, the more worthless I became in his eyes. Right from the start, he didn't want anything from me, except to play games, and I was too blind to see it. Perhaps he was trying to build up some love around him as he couldn't create it within himself.

After finishing my tartlet and a few stretches, I'm back on my bike. I'm almost irritated by the splendour of the surroundings. I'm tired – my body tells me this by sending slightly negative signals to my brain, which transforms them into annoying, and quietly destructive, thoughts. All this scenery needs to be recorded in my mind, as I pedal. I must live it and admire it at 15 kilometres an hour. Appreciating the moment is hard today. I pass the surreal and romantic ruin of the Pont-Rémy chateau. I encounter waterlilies. Ducks. Aforementioned. Little houses in red brick, light blue wood, corrugated iron, all nestled together alongside the canal, replicated on the water's surface.

Amiens.

As I enter the town via a tow-path, I come across various little private pontoons, all prettily different, which lead to small houses in the same style as their respective footbridges. The left-hand side is interspersed with well-tended floating gardens which I barely notice, I'm so exhausted. I also feel dazed and disorientated – perhaps because of all this water – and I need to retrace my steps for several kilometres to find my lodgings. Once I reach my destination, I have a well-deserved whirlpool bath. After that, I draw a map of my legs. They could be peeled and used to make pale pink and blue furry handbags with red dots!

It's 7.30 p.m. and I get up to open my bedroom window because I can hear the sky tensing up. I rest on my elbows and watch the rain that's starting to fall, as though it had just been invented tonight. A few drops at first to test the air's consistency, the impact on the ground. Then the deluge. With the lightning in the distance and me at my window, everything is in its place. Like a cat in front of a fire. I suddenly feel so happy to be here. My muscle cream is making me cold, so I go and snuggle down.

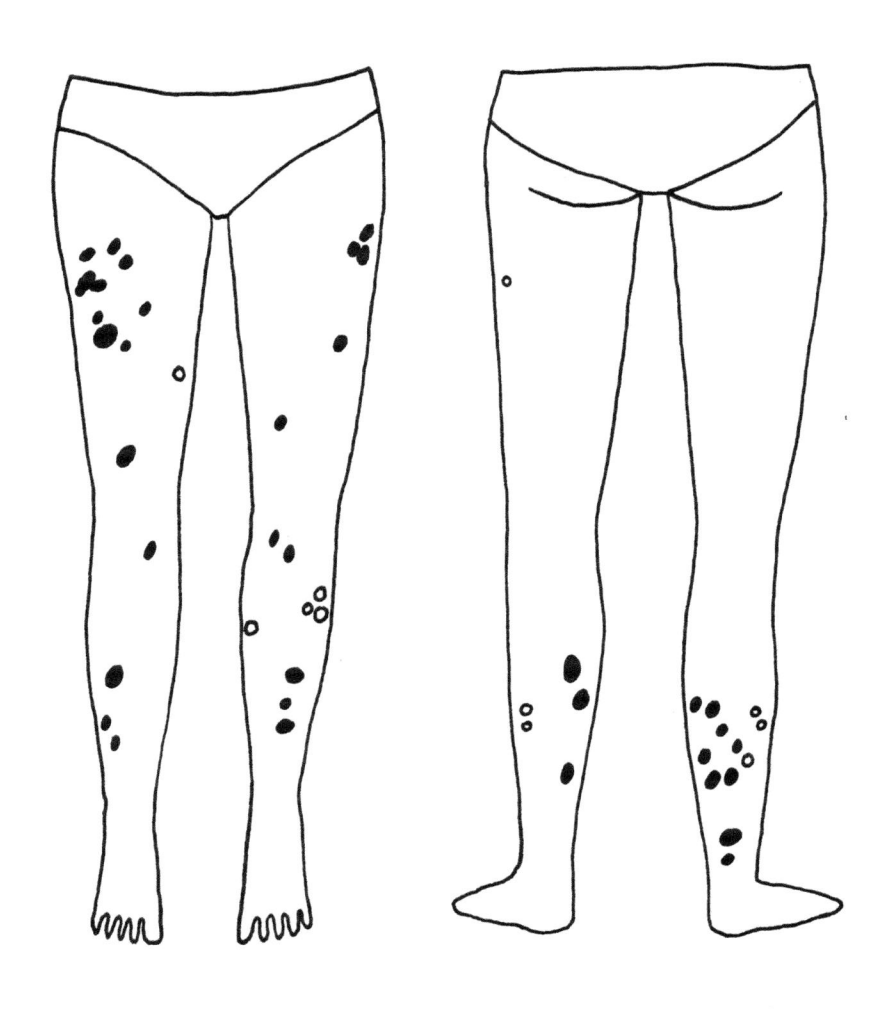

● MY BLUE BRUISES
○ MY RED INSECT BITES

15th October

It's my rest day and I wake up at 10.30 a.m. because another guest started coughing really loudly around six, so I had to start my sleep cycle all over again. Now I think about it, I reckon someone was being sick. I venture out for something to eat and have a vague idea where the town centre is, but I'd like to find the perfect little café immediately. I panic a bit that I'm missing out on all the must-dos and must-sees but, today, even if I just wanted to collapse in the cinema, that would be allowed, as I'm cycling all the way to Switzerland. I'm allowed to do anything. Walking along a pavement in an industrial area, I take comfort in the knowledge that my father has a flair for city walks. You always feel you're where you should be with him, never lost. So I remind myself that I have the same urban aptitude. I've got all day – I can go where I want, and my app works offline as I've downloaded the Amiens town map.

In a narrow little café, I finish my salad sandwich. I push my plate, the bread basket, and other table trimmings to one side, so I can write about what's going on around me. As soon as I begin, a couple sits down at the table to my right and I reduce the size of my writing, just in case they can side-read. My waitress is new to the job and being bullied by her boss who quite clearly enjoys doing so. The boss is a small woman of about fifty with short, red-black hair. She's sporting ochre-coloured suede ankle boots, from which emerge dry, hair-free, tanned legs. She's wearing a red floral dress and round glasses that relegate her eyes to second place in the facial feature stakes – her teeth taking first place. She shouts at everything and goes back and forth for no apparent reason in this narrow eatery. All the houses here are thin and squeezed up against each other. Half the windows on the first floor are optical illusions. The manager barks instructions at her apprentice and checks all the food orders she takes. 'Are you sure she didn't order a *café gourmand*?' Then the lady in charge pushes her fretful way past my table to return to the kitchen, sending a theatrical sigh and forced smile in my direction. I feel I'm bearing witness to her scenes of humiliation. Some women come into the café. The *'Bonjour, Madame'* greetings fly around, followed by the boss's performance. 'Océane, Océane, have you cleared table twelve? Océane, please take table eight's order, thank you!' Her words of politeness have nothing friendly or respectful about them. They're just there to soften the blow. To help the abuse go down. B2 springs to mind again.

    When I was young, my father took me and my brother to a big reunion of remote family members, somewhere in France. I met a little girl there called Océane who, according to fairly vague and disinterested grown-ups, must have been a distant cousin. I was very envious of her name as mine didn't mean anything, and no-one understood it. But here was a great first name: people understood it, it made you think of the ocean, which is beautiful, big, and blue. Hence, it was a beautiful name. But today the name makes me think of subservience.

As I stroll through the streets, my vision is suddenly obscured by huge, intricate, gothic towers. I'm approaching the *Notre-Dame d'Amiens* cathedral. It blows the proportions of my world out of the water. That's the thing about cathedrals. They're always mad, and it's impossible to identify with them if I don't take the time to try. I am a product of Europe, just like this cathedral, so I stop for a while to view it as something that's part of my life. The adornments on the outside are awe-inspiring. You can lose yourself imagining stories about these piles of misshapen human beings. Like a monumental cartoon strip, an ecclesiastical *Where's Wally?* The gargoyles guard the edifice like dogs.

I slip inside by pulling on a door that's named *Saint-Firmin le Confesseur* and which is four times taller than me. It feels like I'm dismembering an entire façade, just to go in. My eyes take time to adjust to the half-light. Then the interior reveals itself and a feeling of servitude comes over me as I stand before such vastness. As I walk the length of the pews, I encounter hundreds of faces frozen in terror. All the characters are ravaged by sadness and worry, and some of them are carrying the weight of galleries or pillars on their shoulders. I don't see salvation, kindness, happiness, or generosity. I'm troubled by the tragedy of human beings who, since time immemorial, have sought happiness, but constantly fail. Here, in the ultimate human construct that focuses on the afterlife, it seems to me that only inferiority, sacrifice, and suffering are addressed.

A German-speaking man, with a little girl of about two in his arms, sits quite close to me in a row of pews. He talks about the round, stained-glass windows in a flower shape, and their colours. The child is spellbound. Her eyes are wide open, as is her mouth. She's absorbing everything. He uses a bedtime-story voice to tell her about the cathedral. The girl points to things that seem important to her and which she feels require an explanation, such as the man carrying a gallery on his back. She directs her tiny finger at objects and turns back round to hear the commentary, her arm still outstretched. Her dad is a story-telling machine. I'm captivated by a tale whose language I don't understand.

I remind myself that I'm doing fine, even though I'm sitting on a pile of people for whom things didn't go quite so well. Raising your eyes, you feel the hope of escape, like a caged bird. There are large windows, and the white light outside makes the colours inside dance. And there are nets hanging from the heights of the vaulted roof. I don't know what they're for, but they're the only thing I find beautiful, because they demonstrate a concrete concern for something, although I don't know what – maybe something falling? Birds that have taken a wrong turn? This soulless object takes on a poetic dimension because of its delicacy in such an oppressive environment. I like the dissonance between these two human actions: the one of installing nets for security purposes, and the other of building a cathedral in the name of an imagined being. Although I reckon hell's reception area could look a lot like this place. Writing that, as I sit on my pew, surrounded by all this pious effort of human labour, a little shiver goes through me.

The class of pupils wandering around this immense structure creates buzzing waves of sound. It's like a motorway that gets closer then unpredictably recedes into the distance. I notice two old ladies praying. That surprises me. Then I'm surprised by my surprise. We are in a cathedral, after all. It was made for that. Sometimes, I wonder where on Earth I came from, but I often feel I have more in common with other animals than humans. This place has no concept of time nor space. Here, everything is distorted. Since work began on the cathedral in 1220, and despite the large amount of redesign due to fire and restoration, time has stood still for hundreds of years, apart from a sign at the entrance inviting visitors to download an app so they can make donations. Perhaps, in this setting where the occasional sounds that do occur scurry away as though startled, we are led to think differently. In a more stretched-out way, between the distant inside and the distant outside. More slowly, too. Whatever it is, this place moves me to contemplation. Have I fallen into the trap? I don't really identify with this bloody and servile narrative, but writing comes easily here and there's no sound pollution, music, or television.

I wait out the time before my appointment by sitting in a little café where I order a hot chocolate. When it comes, it's small and lukewarm. But I've chosen the best seat in the house: a simple armchair that I find pleasing to look at, with dark wooden arms and a square, black metal frame. The seat and back-rest are in corduroy, the same colour as my bike. There is no surplus of material nor design. To my left, there's the large bay window that looks onto the street and, in front of me, a large bookcase full of books that people have left behind. It's cold but I'm warm. I drink my chocolate in one go. Here, I'm someone else. Free from normal life and a financial mindset for a few short weeks. I'm playing the role of a writer-cyclist.

It's almost dark when I arrive for my appointment with the kinesiologist, or kinesiotherapist, or physiotherapist, or chiropractor – one of those, anyway. We talk a lot. I'd sometimes prefer to be quiet, for me to enjoy the massage and for my brain to concentrate purely on sensorial aspects and not on filling the silence with polite conversation. But he's very nice, young, good-looking, and ignorant. I explain that I'm Swiss, live in Lausanne, and bought my bike in London. I can already sense his confusion. We continue chatting. He comes from Clermont-Ferrand and moved here with his girlfriend a year ago. Then he says, 'You speak very good French, though.' It's the first time anyone has come out with that. So I let him know that four languages are spoken in Switzerland, one of them being French. He is amazed. Am I quadrilingual, then? Unfortunately not. Just bilingual, thanks to two mother tongues. I can't take any credit. He's pleased to learn this information and says, 'Four languages! Switzerland must be huge!'

Anyway, he's really good at massage and when I turn onto my back, I notice his biceps.

16th October

Today, I'm leaving Amiens to go to Carole's place in Péronne. The rain is hammering down. I'm over the moon. When it rains, the whole world comes to a halt – people are sad and shut themselves away, waiting for the sun to be fixed. So I make the most of it. I step outside, brave the elements, and get ahead of the others. (Sometimes, if I wake up really early, I get this same sensation of catching up with the universe.) It's as if this 'bad' weather is giving me a break because it hinders other people. I finally get the feeling that I'm not at a disadvantage. I'm riding on the framework of the world, its scaffolding. I'm behind the scenes. I've got nothing against the sun, as it allows many things to happen, but it allows *itself* many things, too. That's because it thinks it sees everything. So it points its finger, it judges. It's arrogant and takes up too much space. I like it sometimes. But I like the rain just as much. The rain doesn't allow *itself* things, but it allows *us* all kinds of things. We can stay indoors and stroke the cat, watch a television series, and read without feeling guilty. Or go out alone into the world and feel it on our skin. It's a nice choice to have. As for the sun, it condemns me when I watch a series.

It's hungry for attention and demands that the whole planet – animals, plants, etc. – go outside and admire it. Rain suffers from bad press. All the better for me, as my goal is to be on my own, and it makes a great ally in that respect.

The rain taps at my face and hands as I ride, rinsing them, and keeps my senses alive. Everything else is wrapped up and covered in Gore-Tex. But nothing is dry, for all that. Under this hi-tech layer, I'm steamed up with perspiration, probably due to the waterproofing. The fresh and salt waters don't come into contact. My own mini water cycle is destroyed by my performance sportswear.

The route is magnificent. It's a waterscape. I think I'm cycling to the left of a stream, then the trees on my right deflate and melt into grass, and I realise I've been riding for ages on a path surrounded by water. It's like I've been pedalling right in the middle of a lake on a thin strip of earth. As I go past, the reeds bow down and at least seven herons take flight in slow motion, then watch me from their landing point. It's proper marshland.

I much prefer this route to the one I took to Amiens, as the wind isn't against me and my attention is regularly drawn to numerous variations: locks every 5 kilometres (sometimes more, sometimes less), riverboats (the same as I see every day and which have mirrored my speed), bends, switching sides of the canal, and changes in surface texture. Boredom sets in when I can see the end of the dead-straight path in the distance, as does frustration when the wind and track surface hold me back. In life, I don't want to know where I'm going, or see the end of the road. I want things to unfold organically at my own free will. A dead-straight road means marriage, house, 2.5 kids, work, sleep, die. I don't understand how this constitutes a fulfilling biological life. How can so many people follow this model? It's forcing life into neat pigeon-holes. And sometimes I'd also like to make my life fit these moulds but, when I try, I feel it becomes distorted. So I endeavour to follow my natural inclinations and meanders in the river. Maybe I'll be eighty-seven before I finally understand this rat-race, the goal that everyone seems to be rushing towards, and then it'll be too late, but, for now, a tree is blocking my waterway, so I have to push my bike to the edge to get past.

As I cycle, all the beauty is slipping away, and I don't know what to do with it or where to put it. Am frustrated at not being able to capture it better. A photo won't do it justice. Something drives me to absorb all the decorative details of this scenery that fly past as I pedal – like a shoal of little fish sucked up by a whale – and then to digest them. I'm not keen on this consumerist and colonial bent. As if being in this beautiful environment wasn't enough. As though I wasn't part of it. My human arrogance would like to own the scenery and store it in a box. Do something with it. I'm realising our creation complex. All we do is create. Everything in our own image. But capturing this beauty would alter it and I would be detached from it. I would emerge from it less beautiful as a result. I go down a slope after crossing a bridge and think of the millefleur tapestry depicting a unicorn that's been hunted and captured.

On this enclosed path, I can't stop myself imagining the video game of my dreams. I combine:

- Natural panoramas: lush greenery, fabulous plants that change position with the seasons, waterfalls, caves, aerial geological formations, special substances like coloured gases that can generate dawn until they dissipate, or subaquatic bubbles made of waterproof gelatine (secreted by willows that weep on the water) that allow terrestrial creatures to build oxygen tunnels so they can live underwater...

- Humanmade constructions: almost Escherian villages (without the eeriness) where there are bridges, stairways, tunnels, secret passages through caves, gutters that can be used as musical instruments and birds' nests. Wooden structures that serve as raised pathways which lead up to the canopy and go down into the river – protected by the gelatine walls – then resurface to go round a mill, and balconies connected over different levels...

- Fantastical beasts: cats, of course, but also oversized, herbivorous creatures that leap out of the water to swallow flying waterlilies then dive back in, and others that watch over the plains, perched like gargoyles on a hilltop, and then take flight like herons.

Every character obviously has their designated pet, their alter ego from another species, their sib from another crib. A journey through different worlds, stories within stories where we meet characters who lead us closer (or not) to the answers. A universe crossed between my old favourite classics: *Zelda* and *Myst*, *Tomb Raider* and *Syberia* with a touch of *Grand Theft Auto* and *Assassin's Creed*, for the majestic scenery, freedom of action and complexity of puzzles, whilst removing the inconvenience of murder* – globally accepted (bizarrely) and even actively sought out.

A thought bothers me: if this moment, this trip, were a video game, I'd be totally hooked on it. Travelling across France in a landscape so real, exact to the half-pixel, where you have to somehow find your way and tend** to your bike's good working order – I'm in. The game would watch over me, because my fate would have been sealed: a path – a narrative arc – leading me to the ultimate solution. If this game existed, I would test everything! I'd take my bike into the water with me, deviate from my itinerary as much as possible, get myself onboard a riverboat, stay with my hosts for longer than planned until they adopted me, cycle through the night, 'pimp' my bike, shag the physiotherapist... Whereas in real life, the repercussions of such actions would be seriously dull... Or downright dangerous. So I settle for having lunch in a kebab shop and finding no clues

---

*   I have never understood the attraction of these dark phantasies. It must be some kind of catharsis.
** I'd like to mix up the French and English meanings – to tend to: look after, focus on, maintain; and *tendre à* in French: to have tendency to.

whatsoever because that's real life and real solutions take longer to materialise.

Péronne.
For several days now, I've enacted a little series of rituals when I get to my accommodation. I arrive like a whirlwind, an erupting human – especially the hair under my helmet – and after my hosts' never-ending instructions (which I immediately forget), I connect my phone to the WiFi and send two messages: one to my parents and one to B1 to say I've arrived. The first is to reassure and the second to show off. Then I do about an hour of stretching. My body is exhausted because it doesn't understand these daily demands and tries to adjust. But it barely has time to get its breath back before we're off again. So I stretch everything as much as possible, even if it means getting into positions that aren't necessarily endorsed. Stretching my muscles will mean they end up accepting their new regime and get bigger as a result, so I can perform better. After a bath or shower, I rub in hot-cold cream for massacred muscles, then finally get stuck into my writing, helped along by a cup of tea. I create a space inside of me. I explore it and discover it's infinite – I can venture into the tiniest nooks and crannies and I'm still safe. Better than the video game as there are no bounds. It's in this space that I'm strong.

MY STRETCHES

17th October

As I leave Péronne with the clock striking eight, the sun is glistening on the water of *La Somme*, the air is cool, and I missed the road last night. I've got used to this flat rhythm, flowing against the current. I sense that my path is deteriorating, and its surface is providing an increasingly bumpy ride, but I'm in denial and remain determined to carry on following my canal, whatever it takes. I've got a headache caused by the way I woke up. Or perhaps because of my shoes. An hour later, I'm on neglected rough ground where my two-wheeler won't wheel anymore, so I have to get off and push it along beside me. Then the gravel makes a reappearance, and I get back in the saddle. I lose all train of thought in the unpredictable melody and erratic clicking of the stone chips rebounding off the spokes and mud guards. An eccentric soundtrack accompanying my travels. In the distance, I can see a tiny, yellow vehicle and an orange man walking alongside. It looks like they're chatting to each other. They're slowly coming my way whilst flattening the bitumen with the road roller. Stopping to let them pass, I see the next part of my route, all fresh and brand spanking new, just waiting for me. I thank

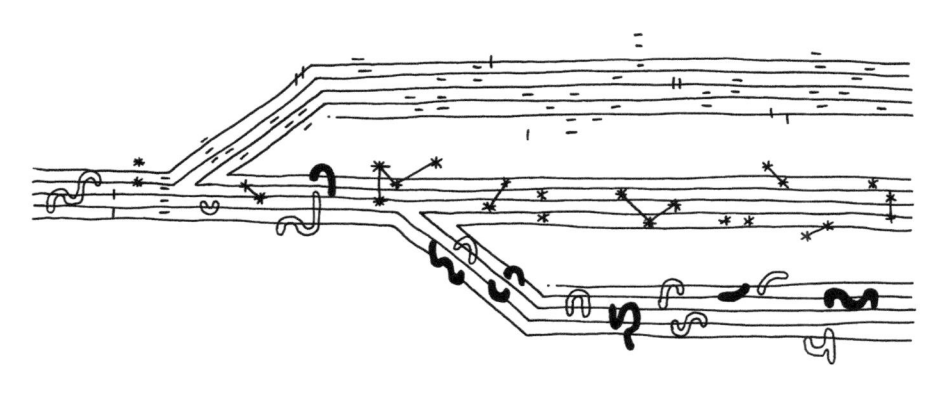

THE GRAVEL IN THE WHEELS SONG

them for doing these works and set off with renewed vigour to test this immaculate surface.

I'm starting to gain confidence in myself and no longer need to keep my phone on at all times for the GPS. Up to now, the route has consisted of sticking to the long Canal de la Somme for 125 kilometres and there have been frequent signposts. So I aim to stop being so dependent on having this well-marked route on my screen. As the ground has become gravelly again and I'm cycling on the right-hand side of the canal, humming the harmonies of that eccentric tune, I notice I've changed direction and am heading too far west. I switch my phone back on. It's exactly at this point that the route I worked so hard to plan to the nanometre was difficult to establish during the preparation stage. It is indeed becoming rather nebulous, and I must admit that my cycle route is disintegrating. I've gone too far along the Canal du Nord, whereas I should have crossed at Béthencourt-sur-Somme, gone onto the east bank, and continued following the Canal de la Somme. I correct my mistake by crossing a bridge further up at Rouy-le-Petit, find myself in a forest, then in some fields, surrounded by wind turbines. When I rejoin the canal, I see that the cycle path is no longer a cycle path, so I leave it to find an alternative route.

Tergnier.
Today, I cycled over every possible substance: earth, grass, sand, mud, muddy sand, pebbles, fresh bitumen, cobblestones. I arrive at my host's place dead on time where she gives me a warm welcome. All this cycling is making me very punctual! There's no chair in my room, nor table to write at, but an array of at least a dozen different teas in an over-decorated box, as well as some miniature sweet treats, all individually wrapped in plastic. I make myself an Earl Grey with sugar and have a mini-madeleine cake that I put on the only bedside table there is, to the left of the bed. It's my comforting and routine afternoon snack. I sit on the left-hand side of the bed next to the bedside table and take out my notebook. Then I realise there's not enough light for writing as the window is to the right of the bed. I push all the things that I'd arranged on one side of the bed to the other side and set up camp on the right. But now I no longer have access to my cup of tea, which is all the way over there, on the left. I continue this absurd dance for a few more minutes until Clotilde, the mistress of the house, knocks at the door and invites me to eat with them. Worn down by this circus of mine, I dither for some time in front of her, because any external strain at this stage takes its toll on me. Then I give myself a virtual slap and accept,

forcing a smile. Once the door has closed, I resolve to swig my tea on the left, then roll over to the right to reach my notebook. My body is done in. I'm beaten by both pedals and pen.

My legs are in a stiffening stage, so I go out for a walk to thaw them out and admire the setting sun. I don't take my phone and allow myself to wander aimlessly around the flat and rather dull streets near the house. Moving with the force of my legs alone – without my habitual metal structure – turns out to be more difficult than expected. It's like my feet aren't fit for purpose and I don't know what to do with their length and the bendable extensions that are my toes. I move along the pavement as best I can, like a beginner with long skis, and think about B2.

When we broke up, three weeks ago now, I said I was going to write to him for his fortieth birthday, which is today, but I have to accept there would be no point. I want to, of course. I would need an excuse to write to him and his birthday would be a good one, but if I really listen to myself and remove all the interference, I can hear that it would be a pointless exercise. Apart from saying here that I wrote to him. But even here, it wouldn't lead anywhere. Nothing about B2 leads anywhere. I know that, but I often confuse it with infinity.

I remember, a month ago, that B2 and I decided to not even try and call ourselves a couple, as it was so difficult for him. He was uncomfortable with the idea and had been offended by my suggestion of calling ourselves lovers, because he thought it was too casual. So we just agreed to see each other when we felt like it. At the time, I thought it was a great idea – as light and airy as whipped cream. It had been a fantastic day. It was a public holiday. B2 and I were alone at the co-working office with 'A', his loyal sidekick. The three of us were like heroes from a children's storybook. We'd eaten our respective packed lunches at midday and shared what could be divided, chuckling about our favourite topics. We'd sort of decided to go for a drink that evening. But when the time came, the studious silence was back, and 'A' went home to see his two loves – his partner and daughter. As ever, the friendships of the day evaporated into thin air. I found myself, yet again, alone in the office with B2, and in the hope of ending the day together. But as our status had just been revised by a so-called mutual agreement, I knew he wasn't going to suggest anything. Hurt and tired of asking him out so many times, I didn't want to suffer further rejection. With our bubble burst, I went home in a very sad state. The day after had been a lot more turbulent. I had asked B2 how often we could suggest seeing each other, a fundamentally twisted question, I knew, but I had to adapt to our new arrangement and understand the rules. His eyes had looked down on me – reluctantly, I noticed – and conveyed a mixture of disgust, disdain, and fear.

    I already no longer understood our relationship. What had we decided? Had I made my voice heard in this decision? What did a relationship like ours mean without any words to describe it? Words like, 'couple', 'love', 'I love you'. How could I adjust to something whose substance I didn't understand? How could I play if I didn't know the rules? B2 expected me to unlearn everything I thought I knew. He wanted to deconstruct my world even though he was incapable of constructing anything himself.

I'm always drawn to questioning social norms, labels, and conventions, because a lot of them don't suit me. And as I'm receptive to the world and B2 is part of that world, I lent him my ear. I also lent him my mouth. He put his words into it. Then he shook my life, stripped me of the fruits that fell from it, perhaps to taste them, and I found myself stark naked. He wanted to reinvent my life. I didn't know if it was genius or a form of pathological behaviour. I didn't know if he was the poison or the antidote. Something about his way of questioning everything resonated with me, and I thought he wanted to identify with me, and understand me, when it was probably just a game to him. He saw my flaws, he saw that I was willing to unmask them so they could be talked about, and he tried to twist them. But it always came to nothing, he never got anywhere, because despite my nakedness he kept hitting my core, which was unshakeable.

Once the notion of being a couple had been wiped off the map, an emptiness descended and other, blurry definitions came prowling. Did he want to use words to hide his desire to play the field? It was a shock to realise I was going to suffer with him, and the only alternative was to fundamentally change so I could be with him. I thought I was difficult to love and felt mistreated. Then, punishing myself for being so weak and giving in to such victim mentality, I wanted to reset my narrative and persuade myself that I wasn't subject to his bargaining, that no-one had power over me. Of course, this was just another stage in the slippery slope of my meltdown. I looked at the possibilities: Do you decide to be a victim? Is a victim weak? That's when a sharp pain went through me and I realised that this state was neither chosen nor suffered, but it was a wake-up call. Like the feeling of hunger. My very being was in danger.

I notice I've followed the sunset a bit too far and I now need to go round in a circle to get back to Clotilde's before nightfall. The mistress of the house has made pumpkin soup and savoury mushroom pancakes for dinner. She makes her own bread and offers me a kind of elderflower liqueur, also home-made. Everything is exquisite. She's overflowing with love for everyone. Her well-behaved husband is sitting beside her. She shows me photos of their daughters at university in Canada and in the United States and tells me in detail about travellers that came before me, one of whom was a seventy-something nun who was walking the Via Francigena, from Canterbury to Rome!

Clotilde has two cats, one white and fluffy like a sheep, the other black and shiny like a snake. She's also got Birdy, a little pigeon who survived an encounter with the sheep-cat, the snake-cat being a very 'scaredy' and stay-at-home cat. Clotilde's eyes mist over when she talks about her animals, visitors, or daughters. When we get up from the table to do the washing-up, she makes me promise to write to her regularly with my news.

18ᵗʰ October

I cross rusty little bridges riddled with bolts which look like parts of the Eiffel Tower. Then, on the other side of the canal, a gigantic industrial building rises up, probably agricultural. It's made up of cubes, 3D rectangles, and cylinders, assembled and piled up like cardboard boxes and toilet roll tubes. Several footbridges link the geometric shapes, and windows are few and far between as they're pointless. This type of austere construction makes me dream of a post-apocalyptic world where everything is possible again. These structures are nothing but form following function. There's nothing superfluous, nothing said without something to say. That's what lends them this strange disposition – a cross between touching, threatening, and architecturally thrilling.

After two or three hours on the canals of Saint-Quentin and the Oise, I have to take a small country track, climbing as far as Coucy-le-Château-Auffrique! Once there, I grab my bike and walk along the ramparts to admire the syrupy light that sticks to the bronze-coloured leaves. Then I hurtle down the hill on a mediaeval path which has been taken over by time and crazy weeds, and

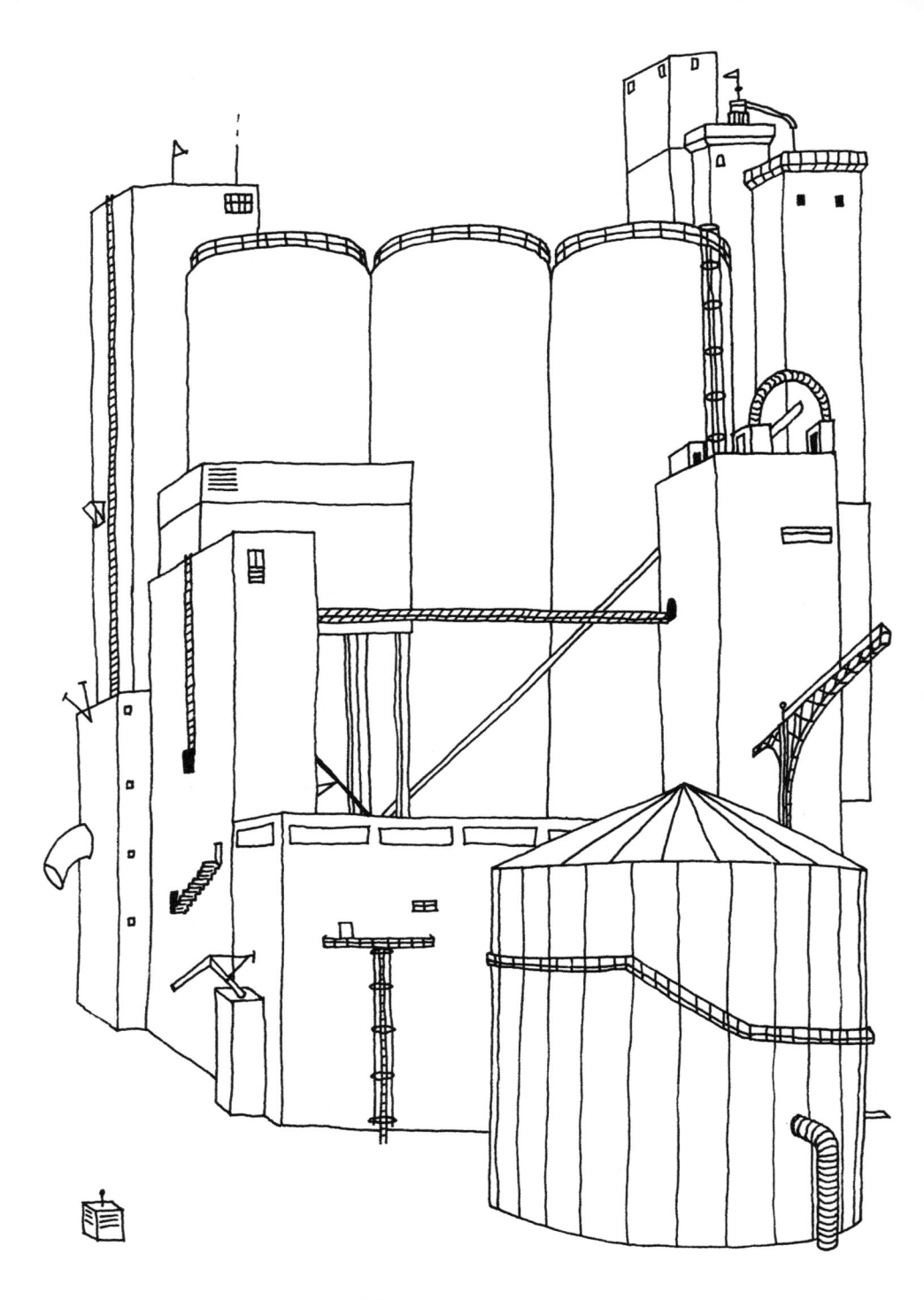

INDUSTRIAL FORTRESS

upon which I endure the underlying cobblestones. Back on the road, it feels like my rear suspension has changed. It has become ruthless. As I get off my bike, I realise it's got nothing to do with the suspension of course – as there isn't any – but everything to do with a punctured inner tube. I hear it breathe its last breath. So there you are. It was bound to happen sometime.

Before I left, I looked up 'changing a bike tyre' on YouTube and found clips showing the front tyre. Then I tested my new skill on my brother's Brompton. As he had an appointment, we didn't look at the rear tyre which takes longer and turns out to be more complicated. Since then, I've remained in denial of this eventuality.

I start by examining my wheel. There's the chain. There's the box and its seven gears. There's the rear derailleur which also reroutes the chain in a double S. The luggage rack and mud guard are connected to this mass, too, and panic wells up in me. I try to calm myself down – they are just parts logically connected together with screws and bolts. It's just mechanics. I can dissect each function from each part, one by one, and work out the solution. But no, it's too late, my brain is already swimming in trouble*. Tons of thoughts explode in my head. If I dismantle this agglomeration, I'm worried I won't know how to go about putting it back together in its original form.

---

* With its 'tr' followed by 'bl', the sound of this word suggests a gentle trembling, the result of an uncertainty linked to the trouble in question and gives rise to an all-pervading blur, tying in nicely with its French meaning of 'haze' or 'blurriness'.

I've got three wildcards at my disposal: look on the Internet, phone a friend, ask someone here. I put my phone on roaming and type 'changing a rear inner tube on a bike' in YouTube. I immediately receive a notification from my network provider, welcoming me to France, telling me they've sent my phone a data bundle of several megabytes, that I'm up to 9 Swiss francs in roaming charges this month and that other very attractive offers can be found on their website, which I can visit thanks to their very attractive data bundles. Once my brain seizure has passed, I come across a list of videos on rear tyres. I start to play one and, during the compulsory adverts, a second notification from my network provider informs me that a data bundle of several megabytes has just been sent to my phone and I'm up to 13.50 francs in roaming charges for this month. I'm reminded that other very attractive offers can be found on their website, if required. The bike in the video looks nothing like mine, so I change clip. A new data bundle of several megabytes – 18 francs. Attractive offers. Another video, this time accompanied by melodic death metal. The 'how to' guide is interrupted by adverts which, in turn, are interrupted by data bundles. At 22.50 francs, I choose the 'phone a friend' option.

My cocktail of pride and shame prevents me from ringing my brother who would probably be able to get me back on the road. I decide to call B1 who personifies my safe place. He's got no idea about cycling and won't be able to help me technically, but I've gone beyond the methodical phase and am currently straying onto the precarious terrain of irrational anxiety. At this point, I need someone to get me out of my stress fog. A few minutes on the phone is all it takes to soothe me, then I contact local garages. My data bundles keep piling up until they reach 45 francs, and the three mechanics who answer don't do bikes. One of them nevertheless advises me to go home, as I can't live that far away.

I push my bike along the roadside for two hours. The few cars that overtake me are heartless, and the speed at which their metal carcasses brush past me is terrifying. Just before Brancourt-en-Laonnais, the road widens to make room for a bench-free lay-by and allows cars to turn round. I stop to perform another examination of my machine, generating several new data bundles.

Three seconds later, two cyclists in heavily-sponsored jerseys hare past me in silence, like yellow-and-black dragonflies. The one behind turns back to ask me if I'm OK. I dare not say no because I'm dying with embarrassment as I don't know how my bike works. But he's already 10 metres away and his head is facing forward again when I reply, 'Er... Puncture!' in a tone calculated to make it impossible for him to flee. He stops. He must be at least eighty. I tell him my rear inner tube is flat and I don't know how to change a rear inner tube. I also mention I'm on my way to Switzerland so he doesn't suggest I go home. He's surprised and explains that his brother, who is continuing to fly up the road in the distance, is disabled and he must make sure he gets home safely. They live nearby so he'll be back in ten minutes' time to give me a hand.

I'm stunned as I watch him leave with his clip-in pedals. This man has come down from heaven. I haven't seen any other cyclists since London and, two hours after getting a puncture, he falls straight into my lap. I shed a few tears of emotion then immediately get a grip of myself to avoid any self-pity. Eight minutes later, he's back and we go onto the grass to give us room to move around the patient. We start by taking off the rear wheel. I suggest I do it so I can learn, but he appears to either want to spare me the bother, or to do it quickly. As he seems very old to me, I think I must seem very young to him, so I ask him lots of questions, like a little girl with her grandfather. I try to follow his movements, his reasoning, the sequence of his actions, but he goes so quickly because he knows what he's doing. I do my best to register the logic of his manipulations and help him where I can. When he's ready to remove the wheel, he vigorously pushes and pulls at it, but it doesn't come off the same way his does. I realise it's a robust machine and won't fall apart in my hands as I'd feared. We then decide to remove the mud guard as the rear wheel comes off backwards and not from the bottom. I ask him if his brother got home safely, and he explains that he fell from a tree when he was young and could have lost the use of his legs forever. He considers himself very lucky to go cycling with him once a week, despite the after-effects. When he's finished, I thank him warmly but have nothing to offer him apart from some dried fruit. He wishes me a safe journey and I watch him take off. In a few blinks of an eye and turns of a pedal, he's gone.

Merlieux-et-Fouquerolles.
When I arrive at my host's, I'm impressed by the building – a renovated miniature chateau, partly adjoined to

a ruin. The estate comprises a pony called Bob, who's insensitive to my charms, some wary hens and a cat who doesn't give a damn. The lord of the manor shows me the way to the bathroom. You have to go through their private quarters. At the entrance, there's a large dog in a small cage. The man tells me it's the guard dog. I don't know if this is a joke, so I say, 'Ah'. I won't be sleeping in these palatial surroundings tonight, but in the caravan parked in the courtyard beneath the garage's tin roof, next to Bob. I dash off to get my soap and towel to take advantage of being allowed to use their marble bathroom. I ponder for a while whether to have a bath which would use up a lot of their water, judging by its oval shape and size, or a quick shower. It's grey outside and my limbs are numb, so I opt for a bath. After fifteen minutes and only a twentieth of the water required, I'm exasperated and end up showering instead, splashing everything.

With a towel on my head, I rejoin the lord of the manor who's watching television with his kids on huge, comfy sofas. As soon as he sees me, he leaps up and stands in the doorway to the living room. His daughters aged three and six follow at his heels then wind themselves around his legs. I ask if I can pop back and borrow some of their Wi-Fi. His reaction is quite peculiar. His gaze remains fixed on me, but I can tell by his eyes that he's slipping away. His body doesn't move a millimetre, which seems a bit restrictive in the middle of a conversation, and his daughters glare at me from their gymnastics station. He hesitates a second too long before replying, 'Yes, perhaps later'. I understand that this is clearly a 'no' in disguise, so I go back to my caravan.

The interior of my trailer is covered in chipboard with a yellow, wooden veneer that looks like plastic. The curtains and cushions are a faux patchwork of white, navy, sky blue and ochre fabric. No other decorative element warrants a mention. Around 6 p.m., the father goes off in a big, black SUV with his little girls. He leaves the dog behind, which barks. Deprived of Wi-Fi, I turn the heating up to maximum because it's getting dark, and my heart feels cold. It's the first time I've felt miserable on this trip. I get out my supplies and devour them in one go: sliced bread that lasts for generations, lemon hummus, a vegetable that's a cross between broccoli and Chinese cabbage, nuts, and dried fruit. There are no tea-making facilities, so I can't even make myself a comforting cuppa. And I'm still hungry. At this precise moment, I'm very glad I didn't choose to camp.

I remember spending a night outside* with B2. The day had been exquisite. We had walked for several hours in the mountains as though on Cloud Nine. Happiness was at its peak – bordering on euphoria – and the scenery took our breath away. Then, when night fell, something had changed. I've never been able to put into words quite what, but I recall a key moment which is still a bit blurred, where I felt a subtle turning point, a disengagement. As if he had suddenly withdrawn himself from our hike to crawl back into his hole. He became softly icy. I immediately felt uncomfortable. I was no longer in the presence of a loved one, but of a threat – a shift that was characteristic of our relationship.

---

* 'In the great outdoors', although there was nothing great about that night.

This feeling didn't leave me all evening despite my tremendous and repeated attempts to get rid of it. In fact, it got worse. The more of an effort I made, the more B2 showed his irritation. I didn't sleep a wink all night. Later on, he was angry with me for ruining our evening and confessed he was disappointed in me, in us. That day, he quietly condemned me.

Sitting at the table in my ochre-and-navy caravan, I stroke my phone screen to view a map of the local area. I find a place in the middle of nowhere called Poilcourt-Sydney. I giggle but feel alone for the first time since I started this journey. I miss interaction. I feel an acute longing to share, I want to create a team of love around me. On Earth, we call it a family. I don't know who I miss or what I need, but I would like one of the Bs to say he loves me. As that's not going to happen, I focus on creating a love bubble for myself, by myself. A kind of self-generated Wi-Fi tethering. I know, anyway, that I lack a bit of fat – not only as padding, but also as a lubricant for life. Because wandering around naked, skin on bone, can make friction with the outside world grating. So I need to fatten up my shield and render it non-stick. That reminds me, when I get to Reims tomorrow, I must pop into a shop and buy some oil for my chain.

Since my itinerary changed in Péronne, my morale took a nose-dive and now I only use country roads, accompanied by cars. I don't really have a choice. What has become of my trip? I'm just following the whims of an app... I'm not in control of much at all and don't feel any of the freedom that such a journey should induce.

I'm not unhappy, just a bit dazed. I don't understand anything that's happening to me, what the hell I'm doing here, how I ended up in this place, and why I'm inflicting it on myself.

19th October

I'm almost ready by 7.30 a.m. and can't wait to leave this austere environment when someone knocks on my plastic door. It's the lady of the chateau, whom I hadn't met before, bringing me breakfast. I'm so touched by her generosity that I give myself an internal telling-off for judging them and shower her with gratitude. A piece of bread, a slice of chocolate cake, cocoa powder with warm milk and some strawberry jam. She stares at me and utters a sterile '*Bonne journée*'. I eat the bread and jam and save the cake for later. Drinking the hot chocolate, I suddenly remember that the *petit-déjeuner* – breakfast – was an optional extra, at 7.50 euros. Disgusting. There's a cafetiere with some ground coffee in my caravan but no way of making tea. They don't think about tea in France. I feel so alone.

I stop off at Pontavert for something to eat as I'm starving after my pricey and very *petit petit-déjeuner*, plus a few scraps from the day before. It's raining ropes*. The

---

* A literal translation from the French expression *il pleut des cordes*, meaning it's raining hard. It's the idea that the water is dripping so fast, our eyes don't have time to make out each individual drop, thereby creating the illusion of one single streak.

young waiter comes to take my order. I go for the veggie burger with chips and salad. 'Thank you, *madame*, and how would you like it cooked, *s'il vous plaît?*' I look up at him incredulously, but I'm faced with an open and honest expression. 'But it's vegetarian…' I say, thinking he'll understand the insinuation. But no, he doesn't, so I suggest it's cooked correctly. The manager serves my food with a *'s'il vous plaît'* which surprises me again and makes me feel compelled to obey an order. The manager is similar to the one in Amiens. She displays a sort of aggressive helpfulness. Each time she walks behind my table, she throws an 'Everything OK, *madame*' at me with no hint of a question, its tempo governed by the marching of her little heels. And the regiment doesn't hang about. As a result, I find myself sitting bolt upright in my chair.

Since I got here an hour ago, ten pieces of generic jazz music have been playing non-stop at a volume too low for legitimate complaint, and too high to be ignored. This trip forces me to forage for detail in one place and the next, and I can't stop myself drawing conclusions from these little pinpricks of perception. Up to now, I've noticed a kind of unease with emptiness. Visual and audial. So people furnish and fill every space, adding adornments wherever they can. They favour 'jazzified' tunes and the decor that goes with them. My body turns cold, so I pay, leave a tip, and go and find my wheels in the rain.

There are fields along my route. In one of them, there's a very sad cow which I stop in front of. She stares at me for some time whilst her cowmates are further away, chewing the cud in chorus. She turns her head slowly in their direction, contemplates them anxiously, then returns her gaze to me. I don't know how I feel at the moment. If I'm OK or not. I can feel plump tears beginning to run down my face and the rain immediately comes to join them, so they go unnoticed. Further on, I cycle alongside heaps of sugar beet, temporarily jettisoned at the roadside, as though swept there. I encounter another industrial structure beside the water which makes me think about video games and urbanisation again, then there are mushrooms like white waterlilies in the grass, a sheltered ruin next to a botanical garden of medicinal plants, and rowers in an 'eight'.

Reims.
I dump my things at the youth hostel in town then head off to a bike shop in Tinqueux, just outside Reims, for a check-up. An apprentice comes to my aid immediately and examines my bike from all angles. He's a young man with a blond bob and nicknamed Kurt. He's got a serene face and a Hobbit-like body. He goes over everything for an hour and a half whilst his superiors ask me questions, clucking like cockerels in a farmyard while its solitary hen pecks peacefully in the distance. One of them is accompanied by his ten-year-old son who's lapping up all his dad's dirty and narrow-minded jokes. I watch this kid learning one hell of a lesson in masculinity... Shit, here's yet another budding little sexist in the world. Due to my sloth-like ability to whip out witty ripostes, I let it pass. I convince myself that if I open my mouth, they'll

take it as a gratuitous attack, reinforcing the cliché of the aggressive female and thus perpetuating the intolerable role dynamics that accentuate the gender divide. The patriarchy is in no danger of being toppled by my sense of repartee today.

    Kurt remains calm and ensures my brakes aren't touching the tyres – just the wheel rims – and tightens them a bit for better sensitivity. He measures my height, raises my saddle accordingly, adjusts the angle, and that of the handlebars, spins the wheels a few times to check what he's done, and concludes that the whole thing had been put together in a rather rushed and rickety fashion. He's amazed I've come all this way without any hitches. He lifts his head and says, 'Good job you're only doing a trip across the globe and not nipping out for some bread on that bike!' It takes a split-second for our brains to compute this comical little outburst, then everyone chuckles. While my apprentice continues his expertise and I watch and learn, the cockerels show me cage pedals that I simply must have, then they announce that Kurt is going to ask me out for a drink tonight. I don't react to their bizarre display of surrogate seduction and, to my great relief, neither does Kurt. He's probably used to working with these blights on society. I leave there happy that my bike has been in good hands. The road whizzes by beneath my feet nestled in their little cages.

    In the restaurant that evening, the music is playing on a continuous loop and the windows covered with an opaque sticker prevent me from seeing outside, so I order my first glass of Champagne since my arrival in the region. I don't really like the stuff but it seems like a rite of passage – it's geographically expected and imbues me with the illusion that I'm in charge of my life. I receive a message from B1 who's impressed by the 448 kilometres I've ridden so far. I've got just over half to go.

20th October

I set off this morning in torrential rain, covered from head to toe in Gore-Tex. I'm particularly keen to test my new bike, following its medical check-up in the operating theatre last night. But after a few hundred metres, my right knee starts to grind. I carry on for 2 kilometres, changing position to see if it helps, but no, it refuses to co-operate. I can't ride like this. In a real state of irritation, I stop. This is upsetting my itinerary, as well as me. I have a think. It's Sunday, the town is lazily coming to life, and the first marathon runners are beginning to pepper the streets.

I spot a Red Cross tent with about ten people in front of it, smoking through a gap in their sponsored hoods which are tightened as much as possible. I approach them in my cosmonaut attire, explain I've got a painful knee due to cycling, and ask if I could make use of their encampment by having a consultation. Flattered, the whole team gets to work: some of them gather around my bike to keep an eye on it, fags pause mid-way, and I hear, 'Damien, there's a lady here who needs to be seen – can you tell the others?' A minute later, a man stubs out his cigarette and lets me into the tent, shouting, 'Marianne, there's a lady waiting, you know! A patient!' To which Marianne replies, 'And?' as she sees me enter. She tells me he could just as well have taken care of me himself and orders her trainee to examine my knee. The trainee, who can't be eighteen yet, looks at her boss blankly. Three of them eventually busy themselves with taking my personal data, feeling my joint, and asking me about my journey. All at the same time. They ask me twice to spell my name and a teenager who's drowning in his hi-viz vest reads out a list of questions and makes a note of my responses, right up to the date of my last period – which I obviously don't know, but he needs an answer so I make something up. They all seem intrigued by my bike trip and keep saying I'm really brave, especially as I'm on my own. This isn't the first time people have said that, and I struggle to understand the keen interest my adventure arouses in others. They appear to understand something about my trip that still eludes me. Personally, I don't think I would be that interested in someone else going from Point A to Point B. It's no concern of mine.

After clarifying that none of them is a doctor, my team concludes it would be better if I stopped cycling, even if it means curtailing my trip. I leave feeling disorientated. I've got to play the parent with myself and decide whether or not the child should stay at home. One day at school, when I was eight or nine, I had stomach-ache and told the teacher so she would let me go home, as she had previously done with other pupils. She asked, 'Are you ill?' Considering myself to have neither the age nor authority to make diagnoses and thinking my modesty would appeal to her, I replied, 'I don't know'. I had to stay at school.

I leave this so-called medical tent with a scrambled brain, and don't know what to do. My head is spinning: the next few nights' accommodation that are already booked, tonight's reservation whose host isn't responding but which has been paid for, the SNCF train strikes until who knows when, see a doctor, it's a Sunday – everywhere is closed, stay in Reims for another night, pay twice for lodgings, take a taxi to my next destination, risk no-one being there as they're no longer responding, find some Wi-Fi. Everything is slipping away from me and I have to get myself organised on my small phone screen, which does serious damage to my patience.

I can sense I'm entering a state of disarray, so allow myself a 'get out of jail' card – I ring B1 whilst savagely beating myself up for it. I'm craving human contact and social interaction, but I couldn't chat with just anyone. He listens to me in his usual understated, easy manner. He doesn't judge – at least not overtly – and knows everything about me. Well, almost. He helps me see through the confusion and I realise the answer is already staring me in the face: I'll stay in Reims for another night, too bad for my accommodation paid in advance, and I'll go and see a doctor in A&E. As I do an about-turn on my bike, my knee starts groaning again and prevents me from pedalling properly, which helps confirm my decision.

I'm the only patient in A&E. A troop of women takes care of me. Each has their own well-defined role, which they tell me in their introductions and which I immediately forget. The knee has indeed been put to the test but, according to the x-rays, it will pull through! I'm prescribed three days of rest and some anti-inflammatory patches. What a relief! I was scared they'd advise me to put an end to my jolly. I would've been torn apart. It's at that moment, waiting for the diagnosis, that I sense the importance of doing this trip. I therefore decide to have a rest day more often – every three days instead of five – thus extending my time away. My brain can't work out how many days this will stretch it to.

Going back to the youth hostel, I realise that my body is far more active these days than my face, which remains glum. I don't talk because I'm on my own, I don't laugh for the same reason, and this physical sensation of immobility, almost in itself, makes me feel gloomy. So I decide to go to the cinema. As it's the afternoon, I find myself in front of an animated children's film, highly rated by the public. I think it's dreadful and dull beneath its pretence of hand-drawn illustrations. I come out of there feeling disgusted that so many parents are blind to the bogus techniques used to pocket money.

I don't go out to eat in the evening as hunger never puts in an appearance when I haven't been cycling. I wrap the bandage round my knee whilst watching a show on my phone, to sugar-coat the day. From my room, I can hear my fellow guests. As in all hostel accommodation, sound travels but the air stagnates. I'm suffocating.

21st October

When I wake up this morning, my bandage and the mesh holding it in place are all shrivelled above the knee. I'm supposed to change it every 12 hours. I put it on about 6 p.m., so how do I make this work? I wake up at 6 a.m. to change it? This type of minutiae can disrupt my mood if I'm not careful. The details can grow out of all proportion if I don't keep an eye on them, then they gain ground behind my back, make tools, and develop communities and beliefs so they can take over.

As the trains are on strike and the buses don't allow bikes, I'm waiting for a taxi that'll cost 60 euros to take me to Châlons-en-Champagne, my next stopover. This trip is going to bankrupt me. The youth hostel's receptionist lets me wait for my car in a pleasant room with tables, chairs, and a big window that looks onto large spruce trees and other greenery. But I'm already champing at the bit to get cracking with my itinerary and to munch some miles. In this waiting room for travellers at the mercy of the town's amenities, the weather, and their own body, the staff have carefully arranged forgotten books by edition on several shelves. I inspect the covers by leaning my head alternately to the left and to the right. *Les grands chemins* (*The Open Road*) by Jean Giono catches my eye because of its title, which makes me think of my little country roads, and of '*chemins noirs*' by Sylvain Tesson* that I'm dying to read.

One of the things I like best about books and literature is that everything has been decided. There's only one path left to follow, that of reading from top to bottom, from left to right. Each letter comes after the other and this linearity leads the brain like a walker on their tightrope. When we open a book, we open our mind. We are often surprised. Are we allowed to do that? To write like that? The writer chooses their words before we read them, and from that point of view, life is simple. The reader accepts everything. I decide to filch the Giono, even though it will weigh me down a bit.

The taxi arrives late, driven by a man who barks rather than talks. He grabs my bike and tries to stuff it in the boot, but despite what he said on the phone, it won't go in. Without warning, the driver decides to shut the boot to force it. I stop him in full-swing and take the bike out so I can remove the front wheel. He seems absolutely determined to push or pull something, so he starts to hit the axle lever which is sticking slightly. I'm annoyed this man is stampeding over my life and my things, so I ask him to let me do it while he puts my bags on the back seat. The wheel doesn't want to come off easily and I have to give it my all, with the driver spying on me disapprovingly from his rear-view mirror. Once

---

*   *Sur les chemins noirs* is its full original title, and the English translation of the book is called *On the Wandering Paths*.

the bike is in the car, I get in the front seat and he says, with a guttural voice bordering on retching, 'So, is that it? Can we get going now?'

I remind him that he was forty-five minutes late, which is like a red rag to a bull. He speeds off at a rate of knots without knowing where we're going.

Châlons-en-Champagne
When I arrive at my night's accommodation, in the rain, I meet the most adorable cat in the world. She was abandoned by her previous humans without being weaned and has been renamed Cleopatra. She's a four-month-old tabby and immediately snuggles up to me, preventing me from going out to eat. Cleo licks her leg to the point of grazing it, so I take her into my room and we spend two hours reading *Les grands chemins* whilst purring. This little book is yellow and shiny, and the edges of the pages are red. Sometimes, when a sentence stops me in my tracks and transports me elsewhere, I sniff it. I breathe in the dust, the paper of other books it was nestled with on the wooden shelves, strangers from another time. It's like going into someone else's home.

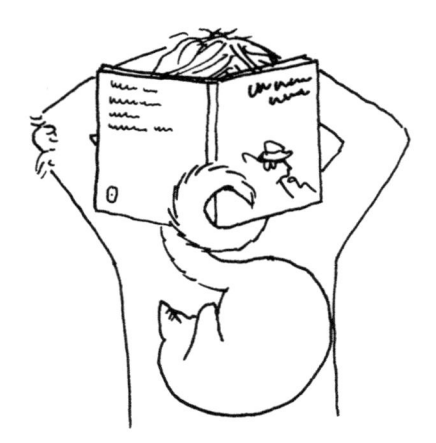

CLEO, GIONO & ME

22nd October

In this house that stretches over three floors, everyone believes themselves to be the boss: Cleo reigns by the simple fact that she's a cat; the teenage human, by his arrogance mingled with ignorance; and my hostess, by her ability to keep them all alive. This morning, I decided to do half of my journey by train to save my knee. Whilst waiting for the only person equipped with a driving licence to take me to the railway station as planned, I hear the teenager overheating because he's lost something essential to his good working order. A pair of GPS trainers or a screen made of foam for all I know. His mother finds the thing and we're off.

The train leaves in twelve minutes. It might be doable, she tells me, lifting my bike and putting it in the boot of her little car with ease. I am stunned and don't understand by what phenomenon this small space seems happy to accommodate my ironmongery. But we're in a hurry, so I don't question myself any further and dash to the front of the car. At the station, I head straight for the first ticket machine I see, a kind of metal kiosk with an iron wheel that allows you to spell the name of your destination by scrolling through letters. I've got two minutes to get to grips with this new technology and catch my train. I turn the little mill-wheel as quickly as possible towards the end of the alphabet: V. I go back up: I. I go back down: T. I go back up a bit: R. I go down to the bottom: Y. I can't find the hyphen. Shit. I try the spacebar. Impossible to identify the destination. Stress. I start again. I try it without a space. Miracle. It knows 'vitrylefrançois'. It ejects my ticket without a sound.

Getting my breath back, I contemplate my bike leaning up against the train window and the scenery that streams past. A mixture of disappointment and relief. When I arrive at the station, I realise my chain is completely stuck in the chainrings, so, to get a better look, I turn my bike upside-down and rest it on the handlebars and saddle. I gently start to pull here and push there, but I don't understand how the rear derailleur is articulated. I find it a bit intimidating. It's like picking up an injured bird – you don't quite know which way its wings unfold, or how its shoulder blades interlock... I get the feeling that if I touch the chain, it will break, that if I move it onto the wrong chainring in relation to the speed shown on the handlebars, my bike will be nothing but a heap of nuts and bolts. I have such little knowledge of simple mechanics – understanding the materials and their resistance – that I don't even know how to test or try something, or just play about with it. I don't know the basic principles. It's a shortcoming that dates back many years and which makes me, in most people's eyes, a normal woman. How come my brother has knowledge in this field – is it inherent? Is he more curious about these things than I am? Was he encouraged to play different games than I was? Probably. And then one thing naturally led to another: he understood a language that I could hear but not comprehend and which became foreign to me. So I associated it with a world that didn't speak to me, that didn't suit me. As a result, I didn't investigate it any further, in spite of myself.

Further up, in the industrial area of the station, I notice a big lorry with a big man inside. The perfect candidate, I think, being crammed with these stereotypes myself. I approach him and ask for help. He excitedly descends from his cab and comes to inspect my bike. He unfolds the rear derailleur like a leg, untangles the chain by rippling it, gives it a hard tug, and that's that!

Getting back on my bike, I'm delighted to see my two landscapes unfurling again on either side of my furrow. But the route is smooth and this foreseeable flatness begins to weigh on me. 'Miles and miles surround me, like anywhere else, but here you can see them'*. I look for mountains. I miss the secrets of their contours, and the unknown. As I cycle, I just try to keep cycling. Once it becomes automatic, I can focus on the water, its opaqueness, the hue of the trees, the herons that take off when I go past, then land 100 metres further on, only to repeat the process when I catch them up. The animals I come across help me grasp the moment, whereas the scenery often gets relegated to the background, like in a photo. Amongst the herons, other animals come and tease me in the foreground, like the Bs.

*   *Les grands chemins*, Jean Giono, Éditions Gallimard, 1951; *The Open Road* (English translation by Paul Eprile), New York Review Books, 2021.

The temperature has dropped a notch and winter will soon be here, which doesn't exactly thrill my grating knee. The colours have cloaked themselves in blue, and the greens no longer exude their yellow hue. I'm freezing as I pedal along and stop every five minutes to pad myself out with an extra layer of clothing. I start with gloves, then my neckband, and finally my baggy pyjama bottoms so I don't crush my knee in its packaging. At the pharmacy – which I easily find because there's one every 3 metres, between each bakery – I stock up on heat creams, cooling gels, arnica, and muscle patches to help me keep going. I cross my fingers. I want to finish my journey on my own two wheels, whatever it takes.

Saint-Dizier.
At my lodgings, where I don't encounter my hostess, I have a very hot bath, spiced with a few drops of essential lavender oil. In the bathroom, there's a pot for earbuds with *I ♥ bathroom* on it. Let's not forget we're in France. But it's still quite disturbing. I turn my head towards the toilet and am transfixed for a second by the paper dispenser which is covered with calming pictures of pebbles and words such as 'quiet' and 'peaceful'. I try to imagine the state of mind required to purchase these items.

Through the large bay window of my chosen restaurant, I can see a dark-haired woman going by. The teeth of a black clip hold her bun in place and a few strands of hair hang either side of her fringe. Seen from this angle, she looks like my mother. I feel as though a large expanse of water is beginning to swirl around my rib cage. I miss her. When I left, my mum asked me to send her a message every day, which isn't like her. She's never been a mother hen. So a part of me likes this new concern that is probably manifesting itself with age. Our text messages are breaking new ground in a mutual connection that doesn't exactly fit with our relationship as it stands, but perhaps with one we'd like to have.

23rd October

When I set off this morning, I realise after about 15 metres that something's not right. I stop on Saint-Dizier's pavement – there are probably others, but this is the only one I know – to find the root of the problem. A lot of cars go past as well as pedestrians. I meticulously spin my wheels in one direction then the other, giving the impression of scrutinising the apparatus and of drawing useful and constructive conclusions from the assessment. Then, fed up with worrying about appearances, I go back to the garden of my B&B to focus on the issue, away from prying eyes. These glances, which in actual fact see then instantly forget, make my sense of deduction disappear because I turn them into a common vision – transmitted from person to person – and into a collective judgment.

The brake is pressing hard against the front wheel. I don't really know why, but I take the wheel off. Probably to dissect the problem. I ponder. I walk around my machine. I examine the situation up close and from a distance. I put the wheel back on. To screw it in place, I first tighten the bolt, but the lever is now impossible to fold in. I push as hard as I can, but to no avail. I spot two workers on a building site opposite. I go over to speak to them, decide against it and retrace my steps, try again to close the lever, but nothing has changed in my brief absence so I go over once more and continue this merry-go-round until I remember that I can just unscrew the nut to reduce the pressure on the lever. The wheel is now finally in place and, miracle of miracles, the brake is no longer touching it! Pure mechanical chance! You take it off, you put it back on – it changes everything. Like turning your computer off and on again. No-one knows how it works, but it does. I keep tinkering with the brake – its angle, distance from the rim – until I find a position I'm satisfied with.

Riding along, I feel happy again. I hum to stop myself thinking about my left thigh which is compensating for my right knee. Cycling beside my quasi-daily canal and leaving room for benoîtesque babblings, I am gripped by a feeling of familiarity. Over the past few days, the horizon has mastered origami to introduce some contours to the landscape. The scenery is beginning to resemble that of home and a new challenge presents itself: climbing. Thanks to shortening my stages, I have more time in the day to write, and to read the Tesson I bought yesterday in a little *bragard** bookshop. B1 was disappointed to hear this as he'd planned to give it to me on my return. That touched me.

The sun made a reappearance today and the yellows are back. I'd almost forgotten this tint which is, however, essential. The colour of joy.

---

*   The demonym of Saint-Dizier inhabitants.

Chatonrupt-Sommermont.
I arrive earlier than expected at my accommodation and this seems to disrupt my host's schedule. At midday, she invites me to have a beer with her boyfriend whom she plans to move in with next month. In the afternoon, I sit down to write at the table on the large patio and, as I never know what day it is, look at my phone. Finding out immediately gives colour to the day. It can darken or brighten it. Wednesdays are rather dull but they're a sign of something good to come. I like Wednesdays. Things are already underway, and the comfort of routine settles in. Thursday is far more boring but at least it's a neutral day, a blank day. Friday slips past, bedazzled by Saturday, in turn threatened by Sunday, who doesn't mean any harm to anyone but doesn't bring the house down either. Tuesday is the worst. It hasn't got the freshness of Monday, which can be biting of course, but it allows you to rethink and reinvent everything. Tuesday is when you realise you're perhaps not going to manage to do things your way and you're going to have to conform. The darkness of Wednesday, passed down from Tuesday, dissipates in the afternoon and we begin to get back on track.

    When my host's black cat comes to wind itself around my calves, I look up from my notebook and, amongst the purring of human activity emanating from the village, I suddenly hear a voice that emits a sound like 'nao'. My heart jumps. But it's not for me. Disappointed, I remember the life I've got back home, where people know me and my name. Some of them love me, too. B2 never used my name. Because nothing was defined between us, hence our dubious status. He never used my name, apart from during our break-up when I cried in frustration, because I still didn't know what I had been to him. So I deduced that I was simply the girl he had slept with for a while. To which he retorted, 'No, Naomi, no...' It just didn't ring true. Like a polite form of address after six months of an intimate relationship. It was probably only the second time he voiced my name without it being part of a joke.

In the evening, my host invites me to share her meal. I'm thrilled because I'm dying of hunger and am out of supplies. She heaps all the ingredients into a cooking pot with some salt and pepper and twenty minutes later, we're at the table. We chat about our lives over a glass or two of wine. After spending eight years in the Army, she retrained and now works in a social services centre for disadvantaged children. I have to stop myself from eating the portion she's planned to keep for tomorrow. As we're both of the same generation, I suggest we use the informal *tu* instead of *vous* (the polite form of 'you'), as it seems less complicated to me. Sometimes, using *tu* helps me relax in social situations. She replies, 'It'll come...' and turns away to do the washing-up. I offer to help but she seems uneasy being in such close proximity to me. She says I shouldn't do the washing-up because I'm not in my own home, and she probably won't use *tu* with me, as that only happens with certain people. I realise I'm dealing with someone who has to actively armour themselves to protect their privacy. I've already encroached on it too much, so I retreat to my room, followed by the manic black cat.

That night as I'm falling asleep, I think about the polite *vous* form again. I would never want it eliminated from French. I like it because it stretches our language by adding a degree of finesse, which allows human relationships to exist in various forms beyond the exchange of words. In a social context, I tend to prefer the informal *tu*. In professional situations, I like the subject to be raised so we can consciously decide on the form of address to be used. If someone asks me in a café or shop, 'Are *tu* paying by cash or card?' it annoys me. I'm uncomfortable with this mock show of affection and conviviality. If you have to pretend, it means something is missing, it means friendliness plays no part in this.

24th October

The sun skims over the countryside and trees disrupt its path. Shadows form black hatching across the landscape. My tarmac furrow weaves its way through the amber rays. I make a pit-stop in Froncles for lunch in a restaurant where all the other diners are elderly locals chatting about the latest news stories. The subjects vary from football – their words played out on a television screen – to something about a woman killing a wild boar. I don't know if I've understood properly. Maybe they're talking about a hunt. I do in fact hear gunshots every day. I eat an entire set menu – starter, main course, cheese, and dessert – for 12 euros. When I set off again, I try to go easy on my knee by riding slowly. That's when I notice the enormous beast lying at the side of the canal path. The wild boar is intact and fresh. I can't stop myself emitting a sound of awe as the animal is such an impressive sight*.

* Questions come thick and fast: if this animal was hit by a car, it should be on the road and not on the pathway on the other side of the canal. So how could someone have moved such a heavy weight as far as here? And why? It will only make it more difficult for the animal disposal unit that comes to collect it. But then, if the wild boar was already on the narrow canal path, what vehicle could have inflicted this fatal blow? And at what speed?

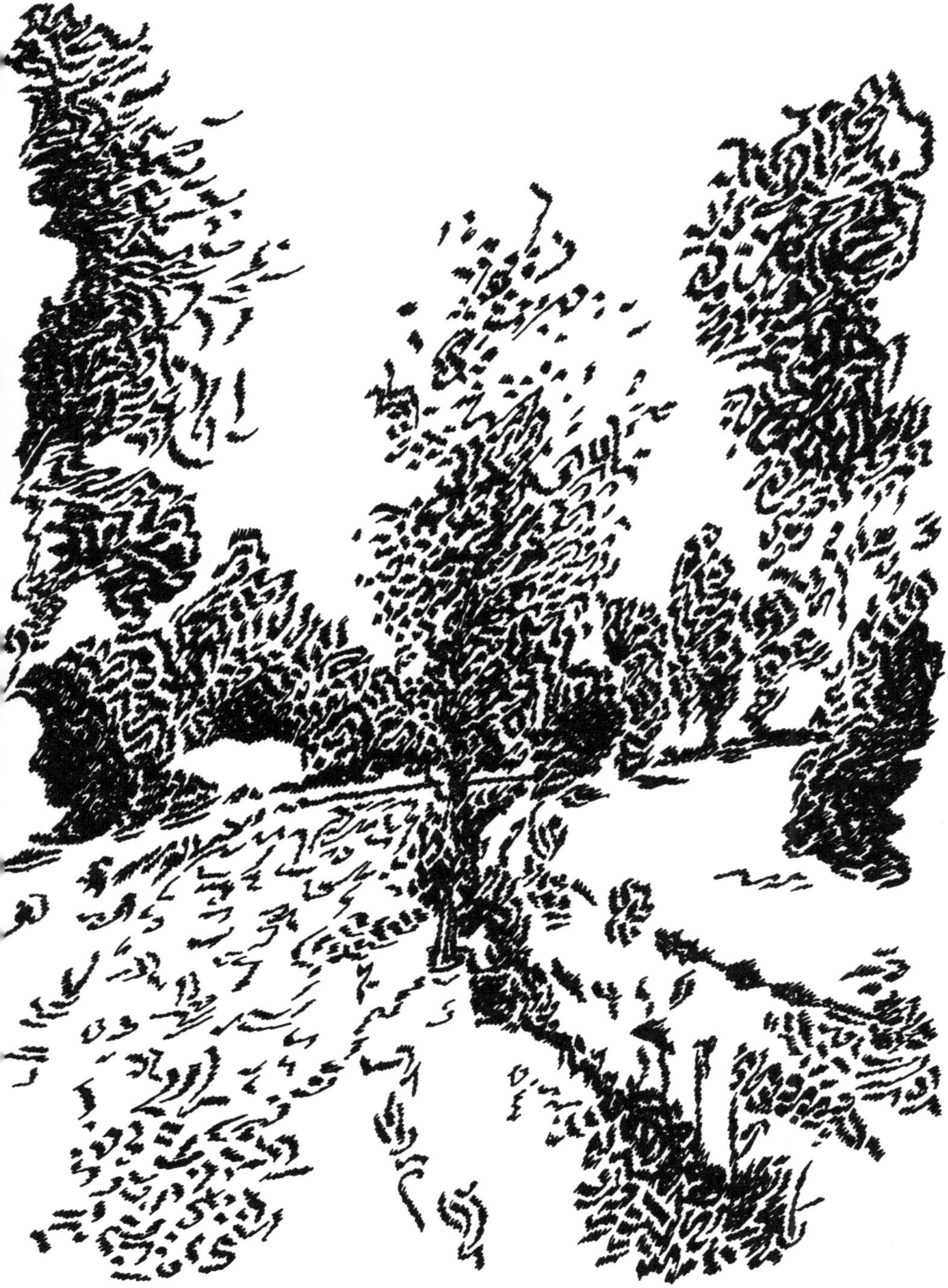

Since the beginning of my journey, I've only used maps on my phone and not physical paper maps. Reading Tesson's book, I feel bad about it. The problem with digital maps is that the hierarchy of place names disintegrates when you zoom in. Information is lost in swipes. But they also mean I don't have to stop at every fork in the road to check my position. I'm nearing the finish line, and my knee starts playing up again. I don't know if it's 'geo-psychological', but I feel I'm getting close to home.

Chaumont.
I glide down a deserted and very clean, narrow street, which seems to have had all the air sucked out of it. A bit further up, two figures are engaged in the tragic dance of a young couple's quarrel. There's a softness to their argument which is fresh from a shared pain. An accusation, she walks off, he holds her back, they cling to each other like a refuge in the distress they've created together, she retaliates, he retreats, and everything kicks off again. The girl's long, fine hair goes wild when she flees, then calms back down when she retraces her steps to give her parting shot. Two seconds later, I'm level with them and have upset the symmetry. She flashes her eyes at me. It's a look full of tears, alarmed at the harshness of love. She's a child in a woman's body. Her image remains imprinted on my eyelids when I blink. Strangers who cry outdoors are a hard and stark burst of truth. Reality markers you sometimes come across.

My body is stiff when I reach my destination. While I wait for my accommodation to be ready, I find a table in a very alternative café that serves tea. Whenever I move my knee, it crunches. I feel like a crumpled, wet ball of paper struggling to smooth itself out and dry off. I do a few stretches, ensuring all my positions are inoffensive in this place where normal people don't tend to wriggle and writhe.

The Chaumont house where I'm staying tonight is different from the others I've seen on my travels. Items were chosen in a far more studied manner. Everything was conceived at the same time, like a work of art, a pure product of fashion, without considering the evolving quality of life, its organic attributes. This house is pretty enough, but all I see is Pinterest.

I choose a restaurant a stone's throw from my lodgings. The lighting creates star-shaped shadows, in duplicate and triplicate. I'm seated on my own at a mediaeval banqueting table in solid walnut. It's perfect. The temperature is ideal, and my chair is a delight for my buttocks. This journey is a strange mixture of luxury and misery. I'm served food by others almost every day, yet my clothes reek of sweat.

25th October

Tesson is right about technology – it's a 'substitute' for life. Perhaps that's why I don't really understand what's happening to me. It's as though everything were going too quickly. Or too slowly. The frequency doesn't seem to match mine. As if someone had knocked me out, then I suddenly came to and carried on with my journey as best I could, stunned. I'm not entirely here and wonder if it's because of my phone. If I'd gone away with nothing but paper, would I be more connected to this story I'm living? And if I wasn't making a story out of it, would I live it more? Or less? Maybe I'll relive my journey fully in a few months' time when I re-read what I've written.

I finish my cheese salad and order a *mi-cuit* chocolate dessert. On my cycling days, I pedal through fantastic and idyllic landscapes that billow like a cape. Then in the evening, when I come to a halt, everything else does, too, because the scenery has disappeared. I ricochet from one bedroom to another, from one denial to the next. The only parts of me that really remember are my muscles. As for my brain, it's on a sabbatical... My dessert arrives, swimming in a pool of cream-coloured liquid. A woman of about fifty-five places it in front of me with the habitual '*S'il vous plaît*'. It's the same lady as in Amiens and Reims. Her eyebrows are worn in a constant state of elevation, her skin is lightly tanned by the sun and her lips have become dry with time and anger. Her man is partly to blame. He's arrogant, and the pair of them have been in apnoea for decades, submerged in the belief that he's dominant. But in the depths of her being, right at the core, she hears something in the distance that doesn't ring true. She dreads opening the floodgates for fear that the tidal pressure will destroy everything in its path.

A group of people comes into the restaurant and the air they bring with them thickens when the door closes with a sigh. The space takes a while to readjust. The external cold and the group's respective aromas are swallowed up in my chocolate dessert. I pay and leave. Outside, a man bellows into a megaphone. '*Mesdames, messieurs*, take advantage of this offer now, at Intermarché, Lidl… What are you waiting for? Come and win a holiday in Sicily…' My eyes dart in all directions to try and locate the stand, but there's no-one to be seen. It turns out Chaumont is equipped with loud-speakers that broadcast the radio in its streets. So I walk around, condemned to hearing a bloke fill his airtime with words he shouts half the time in an effort to retain his listeners' attention.

26th October

As I set off this morning, the air is opaque, as though charged with pale matter, foamy chalk, which allows me to see the white circle of the sun without blowing my retinas to bits. The light fluctuates between orange and mauve. At times when I'm cycling or walking in the afternoon, I raise my head and force myself to really feel this journey, this experience. Then, slightly disgusted by this ridiculous effort, I tell my brain to shut up. In actual fact, what I'm asking of myself is simply to live in the present moment. But, of course, pestering my psyche with reminders to live in the present moment isn't the right way to go about it. So I try and link things to things, internally, to stop them escaping. I trace a thread between the cloud and the stone, between the starling and the ant, and between the puddle and me. Perhaps the only way to understand and appreciate this journey is to stop and stare for a while, just long enough to become aware of the moment, then file it away so I can access the memory whenever I wish.

Langres.
To get there, I have to climb a long slope studded with detached houses, divided by well-maintained hedges. The

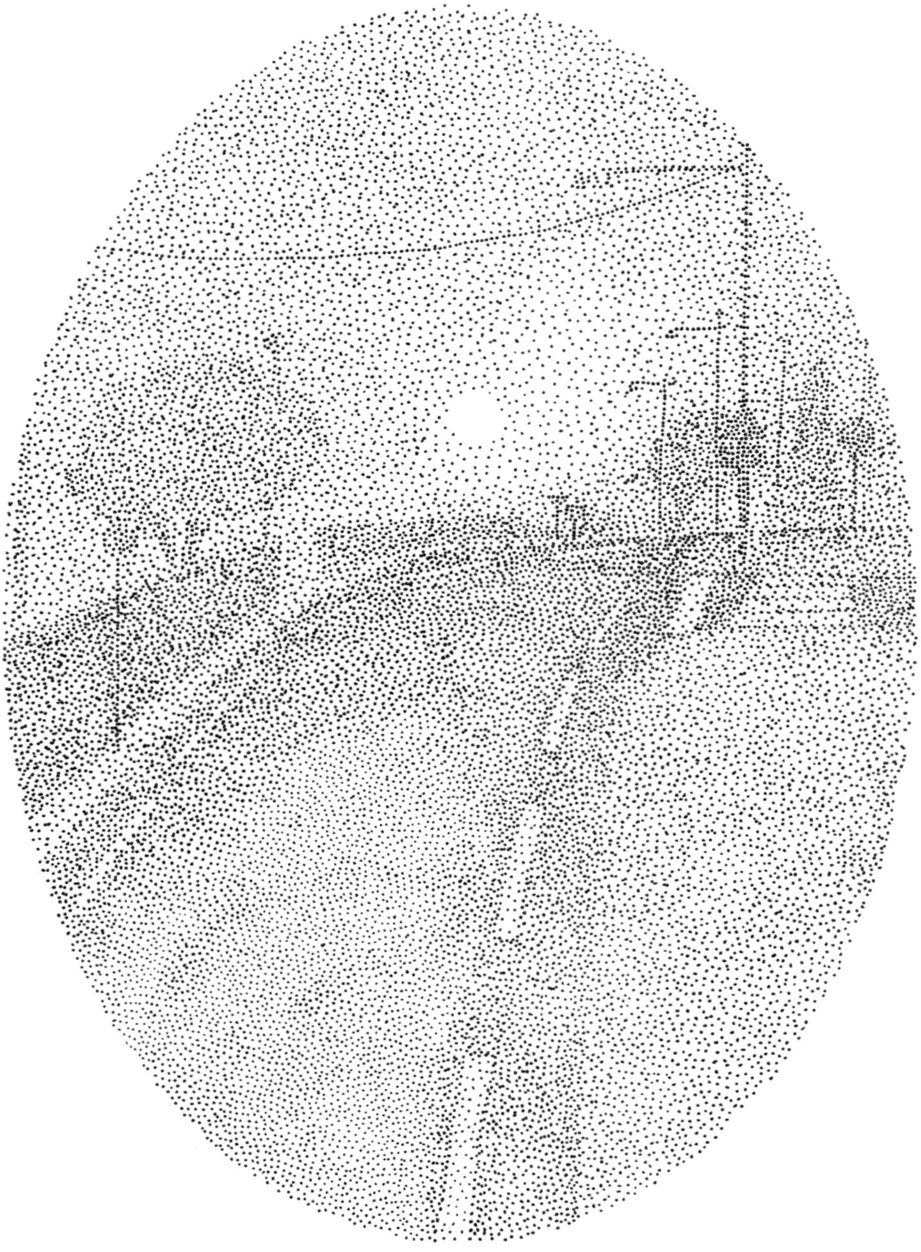

town is perched up above, surrounded by its ramparts, and was previously served by the first rack-and-pinion railway in France. I lose myself in the narrow streets of Langres this afternoon while waiting for my film to start at the cinema. In the evening, I eat three-quarters of my provisions, gazing at a mythical sky.

The house I'm staying in tonight was built the wrong way round. You go in at the bottom with your back to the phenomenal view of the whole of eastern France, then you come out onto the terrace wedged against – and partly under – the cliff. I don't get to meet the family who lives here but can only imagine the chaotic atmosphere and disjointed relationships. Every millimetre is occupied by an object that was acquired accidentally and left there when the attention of the guilty party was elsewhere. On my bedside table, there is: a Pikachu eraser, a red plastic clothes peg with a seriously rusty hinge, a coat-hanger, a mosquito spray, an empty SodaStream bottle, a candlestick holder in which there's another peg (blue this time) as well as used matches – no candle in sight – and three different types of battery, one of which is inserted into an unidentifiable charger. The bedside lamp has migrated to the floor. On the living-room walls – orange and yellow like a sunset interpreted with a sponge – there are lots of adhesive murals of feminine figures carrying pots on their heads, interspersed with several stickers of the latest Disney characters. On the ceiling, there's an optical illusion showing two children tearing off the layer of plaster. Am happy to be staying here just one night.

27th October

My journey is a corridor. I don't stop, except for the night in my pre-booked lodgings – an airlock of controlled collapse. Then off I go again along the GPS pathway. 'The very landscape itself had become the mere scenery of passage'*, and I no longer know if I'm a part of it. While there are only 200 kilometres left to go out of the 1100 since London, I wonder if I'm experiencing the right feelings, the ones I was expecting. People had told me, 'This trip will change you, you'll see, there'll be a before and an after, you'll find yourself, you'll see, this will be a turning-point for you.' I'm there now! I'm looking for the point around which I should turn. But where is the glittering 'Ta-dah!'? I'm here now, watching, listening, writing. It's the only thing I'm waiting for! But I see no sparkle. My breath isn't taken away, it's rhythmic. Am I a human who doesn't like travelling? That's not allowed these days, it's even taboo. It would be akin to not liking music, friendship, or water. It's an aberration. Perhaps I'm an aberration. The problem probably doesn't stem from this trip.

* *On the Wandering Paths*, Sylvain Tesson (translated by Drew S. Burk), University of Minnesota Press, 2022.

I forget that I'm forgetting B2. A part of me – or what I thought was mine – is allowing itself to die. I'm not quite sure what I'm letting go of. B2 was the object of my phantasies for months, but we never managed to break through that barrier and get to real love. Every time we saw each other, we had to start all over again, nothing lasted the night. He'd convinced me that the desire to be in a relationship with him was a failing on my part, the result of some deficiency in me. He suggested we take a break, time for me to get over my break-up with B1, itself caused by B2, which basically meant I had to get over the break with B2 to get over the break-up with B1, because of B2... He tangled up my brain cells and laid down the conditions for being with him: we wouldn't call ourselves a couple* and I'd have to be able to stand on my own two feet before being with him**. Seeing other Earthlings panicking, running all over the place, tripping over each other, and getting married, I found these conditions rather fantastic. Then I understood that they were indeed fantastical. What B2 was looking for wasn't sharing, but the impossible, the non-organic, the non-relationship, emptiness. Like a sort of fascination for purity, a sanitised way of life pushed to its limits and yearning for nothingness.

As the pedals turn, I think about love, true love, the fairytale kind you hear about in novels, films, and songs. Is it just a story that has been rehashed so many times we've come to believe it? An idealised image that no-one's life can measure up to, that drives everyone to

---

*   So, to be with him, I couldn't be with him.
** The often-repeated subtext: I was defective and needed to be fixed.

consume in order to compensate for this lack? Have we all bought into the ultimate consumer fantasy? A bit like the promise of a life-changing, 'you'll see' trip. Mine is like a relationship with its ups and downs. But I haven't been on the heady and overwhelming ride of falling in love. How do other people do it?

Is a ride through beautiful scenery all they need to understand the meaning of life? Is that what love's all about? Meeting someone you're compatible with and saying, 'Ah, so we love each other, then.'

Villeneuve-sur-Vingeanne.
When I get to my night's accommodation around 2 p.m. – a farmhouse proudly renovated to look like a manor – a pig, two goats, three donkeys, two hens, and a goose run towards me from behind their enclosure. There are about fifteen animals in blissful cohabitation in the large field adjoined to the human residence. I find the key under the mat and go inside this homestead where rooms are far too big for normal furniture. It's like being on the sea-bed where everything has gently fallen back to the floor after a visit from a predator. Still and peaceful. I get settled in my room and begin stretching when the cat of the house comes to introduce itself. It immediately curls up into a ball on my pillow. Next, I eat nearly all of my reserves apart from the banana which I keep for the morning. I'm still hungry and can feel gloominess lurking, so I go out for a walk. I spend forty-five minutes going round all the roads in this back-end of nowhere, walking in slow motion as my legs have forgotten how it's done.

DEEP-SEA LIVING ROOM

The winter hour came creeping in yesterday, like a lover in the night. It's ultraviolet outside and in the time it takes me to write these words, the colours have changed. I'm still hungry, so I go downstairs for a rummage in the cupboards but only find a half-eaten jar of Nutella. I stuff myself with it as I read my Tesson book, intimidated by the elegance of his words. I only just have time to put away my spoon when the owner arrives. I'm surprised to see such a young master of the house. He asks if I want to share a *raclette* with him and I accept without hesitation.

While I'm brushing my teeth, I receive a message from B2 who has seen the photo of my bike on my WhatsApp profile and wonders if I've finally started my cycling trip and, if so, his eyes are welling up and, if not, he'll be a bit disappointed. In theory, his message annoys me because he's yet again taking control of my dreams, my privacy, my identity, in the belief that he's got something to do with it. But in reality, my body switches to another state: everything lights up, my heart races, my brain sizzles. Stupidly, I immediately reply and after two minutes, he's already stopped responding.

28th October

I continue to follow my tow-path along the canal between Champagne and Bourgogne and go under the long and well-proportioned Oisilly viaduct, near Blagny-sur-Vingeanne. I'm 200 metres away from where I'll be spending the next two nights, and my knee has decided to make me suffer in a different way. Now the pain appears more complicated than simple overuse, less superficial.

Ever since Sylvain Tesson started accompanying me on this journey, he has enthralled me at times and irritated me at others. Today, he's irritating me. He snubs snobs. He looks down on people like him, as any good boho would. I find that frustrating as it's a dead-end argument. He mocks hikers in Gore-Tex who follow marked footpaths. And that reminds me a bit of B2, up on his high horse, theorising about everything, convinced and fascinated by his own self. After a month of silence, his little message yesterday has stirred up particles in me that had previously settled.

B2 pretended to want me. All of me. Then, with each day that passed, he slowly pulled at my petals, one by one, gradually stripping me of the interest I'd been led to believe he had in me. He picked through what he wanted and what didn't appeal to him, because others had allegedly used him in the past. By default, I trust people and wanted to see him thrive. But I didn't think it would be at my expense. The further forward we moved, the more I shrank to give him the room he so desperately needed. At the same time, he blamed me for not taking up my own, but I could clearly see it was impossible to fit these two forms into a space like love. He always claimed to be a generous, nice kind of guy, but I never quite sensed the goodness that he was so sure defined him. One day when we were on a walk by the lake, I confessed he didn't seem particularly like that to me, and he fell apart. Perhaps because without this forged identity, he was uncovered. And without his cover, he disappeared...

He judged me a lot on how I looked after myself. We spoke the same language, and were infatuated with the complexities of the world, but we applied different definitions to them. So we failed desperately to cross paths. How he made me dream. Up to the point of exhaustion. In a way, our break-up was orchestrated by him and executed by me. Despite my feelings, but not in spite of myself. Because I felt that, as time passed and the relationship destroyed me, the closer I got to coming to my own rescue.

He'll probably continue to bruise some hearts, but these hearts will go on to repair themselves, whereas he'll stay put, broken from the start. He'll end his life dissatisfied with not having found what he was looking for, as it's obvious he's in desperate search of something. A search which seems quite healthy and convincing from a distance but, the nearer you get, you realise it's abrasive, destructive. That it repels all forms of life. He regularly came up with new theories and preached about them to his entourage, which made him shine socially. Basically, he didn't want anyone, but he pretended to want to bring everyone together, without ever being capable of maintaining a genuine connection, while that was precisely what I was looking for. Always and in everything. B2 liked to surf people. He would meet a stunning woman at a wedding, spend the evening with her, probably slip into love, come back from the wedding and go on in detail to me about this awe-inspiring encounter. I concluded from this that I wasn't enlightened enough to accept all his loves. Now I realise these loves were actually the only ones he could experience, because they exist on the surface and are gone in a heartbeat. But he'll never experience real love.

He said he'd changed fundamentally during a certain period of his life, but he'd just added a thick layer of deception to his little scheme, falling ever deeper into his own trap. He's as handsome and hideous as a character in a tragedy, or perhaps he's nothing at all and I'm just floundering around in my own melodrama. Give it two years and he may have lost all his palatability.

The two Bs have had a big impact on my life, a lot more than the boys who came before them. The first one strengthened me, believed in me, and helped me find a way to shape my life – by writing. The second one gave me such a slap (figuratively speaking!) that after letting him go, I had nothing left to lose by going for it. But he certainly didn't contribute to my development in any way. He was a black hole from which I escaped in time.

Thervay.
My legs are telling me the trip will soon be over, whether I've got to my destination or not. As I sit having a cup of tea with my host couple, my blood circulation plays for time. I'm careful when I get up from the chair. A little glimpse of what old age has in store for me. I could bet on it that Tesson owns a Gore-Tex jacket.

29th October

Rest day today. Relief. I've finally stopped planning all my remaining stages after much uncertainty and anxiety about the altitude that lies in wait. Am in a tiny one-horse town in the middle of nowhere, right between Dijon and Besançon. I wondered whether to go through those towns, as it would've been more exciting, but I'm exhausted and I thought the countryside would help get some air into my lungs before the big climb.

So I go out for a walk. It's 2 p.m. and the sky is so laden it crushes all shapes and erases all shadows. Officially, it's still daytime, but you wouldn't think it. Colours have obediently assumed their respective positions, but the light is suffering from a bout of 'the day after the night before'. I've got the nightmarish sensation of being confined and compressed even though I'm outside. As if breathing were no longer enough.

I entrust myself to the little village paths and suddenly realise a river is coming closer between the trees on my right. I'm piqued with curiosity to go and take a look. A little chain between two fences tries to put me off. I stumble for a moment over this hint of an obstacle. Before I know it, I'm getting out my phone and zooming in on the map to find out what's concealed on this patch of ground 10 metres away. A highly sponsored cyclist goes past and sees me in the middle of a field, in this arse-end of nowhere, gawping at my smartphone. I realise I'm verging on insanity, so I duck under the little chain and step onto a pretty micro-beach on the banks of the Gravellon. Two boats that look like toys have run aground at the edge and are tied up. My eyes actively start looking for paddles and a tool to break the moorings, when I remember my life isn't a video game. I retrace my steps to try and find a circular path back to where I'm staying.

I attempt to write as I walk. The bouncing motion lends itself better to the task than the swift course of a bike because the world undulates at a similar frequency to words. And it's more conducive to survival.

When I leave the path to join the main road, I frighten a colony of starlings which erupt into a cloud, then fold into a tree and miraculously melt into it. Further on, between the pylons, I can see their ruffled-feathered friends on electric cables, clearly angry and in noisy debate.

When I get back, I notice the strange shape of the house – a sort of half-trapezium leaning on its side. Everything here is bleak, including the village name – Thervay. The sky is low and white, like the ceilings. In this house where windows are scarce, tiny, and in the wrong place, everything has been designed for small human beings. The sink and the cooker hob only come up to my thigh. In this huge, squat kitchen with white cupboards on all sides, there's not a single sound, no radio nor television on. Respite. But this kind of silence forces me to control my movements which have become clumsy with wear and tear. Putting a glass down or pushing a chair in requires a lot of concentration, to avoid waking the atmosphere. I don't know if the homeowners are here or not. I can hear my heart beating. I'm sitting in the kitchen because there's no table in my room to write at, and it's the room with the best light. Next to the kitchen, there are two other rooms, also furnished with a table and chairs, so that's three spaces which all seem to have an identical purpose. I suddenly notice the man of the house has come into the kitchen, looking for a cup. He sits down at the same table as me, despite the other two, and tries to position himself so carefully that I'm completely distracted by his shuffling and measured movements. Like a sloth. New humans always surprise me. This bizarre moment drags on, so I decide not to even bother finding a topic of conversation and let myself wallow in the ambient unease. If everyone is aware that everyone is aware of the uncomfortable silence, does it cancel itself out?

30th October

My route changes dramatically today as I leave behind the canals that have accompanied me this far. I've planned to follow greenways and cycle paths running parallel to the road. At 7.30 a.m., I go downstairs for the full English breakfast my host couple has made for me. I'm about to sit down with them at the kitchen table when they point to a place they've set for me, two living rooms away, in the gloom of the third space. I eat in silence, surrounded by a small bouquet, seven jars of jam, and four embroidered placemats. I can just about hear the couple in the kitchen – the door is ajar – discussing various topics in whispers.

    When I'm ready to go, with my bags on the luggage rack and helmet on my head, they tell me how happy they are that our paths have crossed and watch me leave from the doorstep, like grandparents at the end of the school holidays. I'm touched and almost saddened by their tenderness. I set off slowly for the sake of my knee and limbs which are coming back to life after their day of rest. The path begins to warp, and I enjoy this new muscle workout that makes a pleasant change from the flatness of the canals. The sky has never been so low.

Unless it's me climbing into it. I can feel the mountains – their rock surrounding me and reaching upward.

After cycling for forty minutes, I realise my front tyre is flat. I'm in the centre of the village of Gendrey and am relieved not to be on my own for this second puncture. I stop under a roof because the drizzle is pricking at my face. I take the three bags off my bike and turn it over to have a look. I remove the punctured inner tube and change it easily. But when I try and use my pump for the first time, it sticks. A kind of brain turbulence immediately takes hold which yet again prevents me from thinking clearly. I can see three men in hi-viz vests 30 metres away, fiddling with a fire hydrant, so I take my pump over to them and ask for help, telling them I'm a novice. The second they reveal the solution to me, I realise I already had it inside me – forgotten, gathering years of dirt and dust. I just have to unscrew a small nut so the pump can access the air. I thank them profusely and go back to my bike. I check the inside of the tyre thoroughly by running my fingers along it to make sure there are no thorns or sharp bits, then the two men, having finished working on the hydrant, come over and cheerfully admire my bike. They show an interest in my trip and, before you know it, they're pumping up my tyre. I tell them about my first puncture and explain I'd like to do it myself now I've learned how. They're so happy to help me that I don't have the heart to insist. Once they've finished, they wish me a safe journey and go off to examine their next fire hydrant. As I'm putting my wheel back on, the old woman who's been spying on me ever since I decided to set up my repair workshop in front of her house, comes out to tell me her son should be arriving any second with her shopping as he couldn't do it yesterday. When he arrives and parks the car, she invites me inside to warm up with a coffee.

Thirty minutes later, when I'm in the next village and thrilled to be riding uphill, I hear the wet puddle sound again. It's my front wheel. I swear under my breath. I'm dying to go to the loo, so I stop in a courtyard where people are chatting. I explain it's the second puncture I've had in an hour, and they escort me to their bathroom door. When I come out, I get stuck into this new repair. I turn my bike over on the gravel, and a big, teddy bear of a man comes over and helps me without interfering. It's perfect – his presence is reassuring. He asks me where I'm from. We chat away as I perform the same actions as thirty minutes ago. He tells me he's an HGV driver and it's his day off. Perfect timing for a puncture, as ever! I inflate my inner tube to locate the wound and we closely examine the wheel. There is in fact a sharp piece of rock discreetly lodged in the outside of the tyre, which also has a hole in it. I hadn't noticed it during my previous inspection. I remove the twice-guilty offender with my tweezers and begin my first patch-repair of an inner tube, which I learnt from YouTube. I have trouble putting the wheel back in the rims, and wedge the inner tube between the two. I can still hear the soft whistling of air escaping, but maybe it's just my imagination. After several long minutes of faffing, I finally succeed in putting everything back together without any suspect hissing, and I'm pretty chuffed about it (although a little paranoid about the front wheel). It takes me a while to get going again due to my frozen limbs that have aged a good forty years since this morning.

I go through the forest of Chaux on a track that runs next to the road for 8 kilometres as the crow flies, and which has a few changes of gradient. An avenue lined with yellow trees. What a treat for a cyclist! A bit further on, my track comes to an end, and I arrive in Mouchard*. Disappointed to find myself back amongst traffic, I raise my head to read a green road sign and what I see makes me brake and expulse an unidentifiable sound, rather like that of a choking peacock – 'LAUSANNE 119 KM'. I come to a complete stop and begin to giggle and talk to myself. A lady walking past at a distance eyes me with alarm. I take a photo of the sign and set off again, ecstatic. A few tears help me see the road ahead in sharp focus.

As luck would have it, a new cycle path appears. I take it. This time, it allows itself to go a little crazy and deviates from the road. The path climbs a lot higher than the cars and follows the course of the Furieuse river 40 metres below. I go through a tunnel beneath the rock and then cross a bridge that straddles the road. I'm over the moon. This is what I've been missing. A change of pace. I can pin my thoughts, concentration, and muscular activity on this terrain. Everything just glides along when it's flat, including time. But here, the landscape is rugged, and I understand how I'm moving through it. My arms and legs work to hold me in a plank-like position. My little city-girl muscles rejoice.

---

*   *Mouchard* = snitch/grass/informant. The perfect name for a fictitious little village in a murder mystery.

Salins-les-Bains.
I'm not that far away now. The cloud descends even lower and interacts with the ground in mysterious ways. As I enter the town, I spot a bike shop that opens in two minutes. I'm about to do a few stretches to keep my knee going when one of the shop's employees pulls up in a car. I follow him inside and tell him about my double-puncture experience. I ask him to do a check-up and he does it while I voice all the questions that come into my head. He retightens my chainrings and checks the wheel alignment by turning it on an axle and pinching the spokes with a flat little tool. He asks me where I spend the night and what I do for meals. I tell him I stay with host families and vary my eating habits between home-cooked food, restaurants, and my own supplies. He disdainfully mocks my travelling style and tells me that, at my age, I should be pitching a tent and getting by on whatever food I can lay my hands on. Then he says I should have had some chips in Northern France, that I really missed out on something there. I'm annoyed with him for spoiling this victory in progress. I can hear rumblings of resentment inside me. I start justifying myself with arguments of heaviness, coldness and beginnerness... But he's not impressed. I refrain from telling him I'm writing about my journey and that, for writing, it is recommended to have 'a room of one's own'*.

I'm disappointed in myself and put this stranger on my mental blacklist. But it's only temporary. He raises the

---

* *A Room of One's Own*, Virginia Woolf, Penguin Classics, 2000.

subject of my chain and shows me a measuring tool with a kind of hook on it that can tell when the chain is slack. It is actually a bit saggy after 800 kilometres. I'll have to replace it when I get to Lausanne. I ask loads more questions and we're mates again. We talk about materials, steel, aluminium, ecology, and old planes that are melted down and made into bicycles. I interrogate him on the hideous shapes of these hi-tech, ultra-performance bikes. Doesn't marketing have a part to play in these designs that are more Grendizer than pedalling machine? No, not at all, these hydro-formed structures are absolutely necessary. But the information he gives me isn't specific enough, so I push him further and, when he runs out of suitable responses, he just repeats the same things using vague, generic terms. I buy a new inner tube, thank him, and go off to find my 'tent'.

The woman who greets me isn't happy with my twenty-minute tardiness. I tell her about my bike trip from London and my double puncture of the day, but that's not her concern. It's already 5 p.m. and night is falling. The cloud, too. It's collided into us. I'm wrapped up in the mountainsides and this misty cotton wool. Trees and roofs disappear in perfect degradation. The atmosphere is heavy with mystery, it's like I'm part of a novel, and I finally feel that unprecedented freedom I was looking for. A freedom I associate with the dampness in the air caused by rain, with autumn, and with this weather that people call bad. I'm right where I want to be, and all roads belong to me. Perhaps that green sign has loosened me up. It's realigned me, reconnected me to my goal. Like a dog in a car that suddenly recognises its home. I'd like my life to consist of seeing my loved ones for a while, going off on bizarre adventures to places no-one's interested in, and writing. Both my bike and this trip are involved in the creation of an identity – fictitious, of course – which will probably come alive when I get home and tell people this tale. As I write these words in an umpteenth restaurant, I spy a rather cute waiter. Damn, he's not assigned to me.

31st October

As soon as I leave the town, I begin to go up a small road that I share with three cars, which gently overtake me. It's a perfect climb: beautiful, smooth, difficult, and I'm cheered on by the local cows. The fog is so thick I have to switch on my front and rear lights, as well as my head torch which I turn to red and place at the back of my helmet. I can't see more than 3 metres ahead. I imagine Salins-les-Bains to be a magical town that appears and disappears, according to the whim of travellers. When I get to the top, I continue to follow the undulating terrain through fields and forests. The landscape's anatomy seems so manageable that I forget the effort involved.

The advantage of travelling alone when you're using your muscles (and even if you're not) is that you don't have to listen to anyone else complaining. A trip like this obviously generates some physical discomfort and when the other person is hurting, it's unbearable, because other people's whingeing is hyper-bloody-annoying, because you can't do anything for them, and because you don't know how bad their suffering is. When we're in pain and moan about it constantly, we suffer twice: the first time from the actual pain or affliction, and the second time from our determination to express our new torment to the world. Cats, for example, almost always only miaow in the presence of humans. They've learned our obsession with naming and expressing everything in order to produce a change in state – from hunger to being fed.

Longcochon.
When I arrive at my guest house, a woman of my generation greets me at the door. I collapse in front of her then we store my bike away. I put my things in my room and go out for a walk so my body doesn't slip into the stiffening stage too quickly. It's just a short stroll but makes a change from my usual circular movements.

When I get back, I find a spot next to the fire where I can write. I'm alone in the room. The landlady's children are playing outside and making little round, high-pitched sounds. They're one, three, and four years old, and they form word bubbles, they babble and gush, then switch seamlessly to whining. All of a sudden, the words of a text that B1 sent me when we broke up spill into my head without warning – 'I've loved you for a long time. Never will I forget you.' This little snippet of the old French nursery rhyme, along with its tune, still haunts me and triggers an overflowing of emotion. I put down my trusty pen which starts to speckle on the page, and close my eyes for a moment.

1st November

Day of rest in a comfort-cocoon where the host family takes care of me. I'm in heaven. I have my breakfast, dinner, and supper in the dining room, surrounded by hikers and shy tourists who are passing through. It feels like I've found the care home I phantasised about as a teenager. A kind of paradoxical freedom. Some of them go off horse-riding and others leave to continue doing I don't know what in a life I can only imagine. There's a very young couple with a baby. They appear shaken by life and seem to be on the run from their judgmental families, searching for peace. A mother and her little girl. Their attire isn't fit for the mountains and the matriarch corrects everything her daughter says and does. Nothing is how she would have liked. Perhaps she's taking the girl to a remote boarding school somewhere to instil some discipline in her. A retired couple. They're wearing checked shirts by sports brands, they know each other inside out, and are speaking Swiss German. How lovely it is to hear this strange, protracted melody again, punctuated with percussive bursts. Between meals, I write and go out on little excursions in the vicinity.

2nd November

It's 6.14 in the morning. My fingers are limp. Nothing has woken up yet. Spelling and grammar slowly come back to me. Perhaps they haven't actually left, but during the night they allow themselves to wander off and make way for other systems.

In my original itinerary, before my creaking knee, I was supposed to get home today. But now it'll be tomorrow. As usual after a rest day, I'm itching to get going again. So I accept this premature awakening and set off. The sun comes out to play for the first half-hour to warm me up, then the rain comes down in a deluge. I have to blink really quickly to see anything. My eyelids are tennis racquets hitting the balls fired at them.

Chez Liadet.
When I reach my accommodation, I'm frustrated by the small amount of distance covered. I stop for a few seconds in the torrential rain, bike between my legs, and look at my lodgings for the night. The hostel is situated on an insipid scrap of land. Nothing exciting can happen here. I'm soaked to the skin but I'm not cold. I put my right foot back in the toe-clip, get up some speed and

launch myself at tomorrow's route. I didn't think I'd be up for tackling any more kilometres, being in the mountains with a rickety knee.

So here I am, suddenly catapulted into the last day of my journey. I can't believe it. Someone texts me, 'I can't wait for you to tell me all about your trip!' But what will I be able to tell them? A natural reserve surrounds the greatest moment of my life and prevents me from gloating about the joys of this little jaunt. There have been static places, rolling roads, several cats, a few people, my legs and my head. It's the story of someone who cycled their story into a book, and it turns out that travelling is involved.

As from tomorrow, everything will start again. I'll have to expose myself once more to all that's familiar, with my new 'I did this trip' identity. What will I be like? What did I do this journey for? What the hell have I just done, exactly?! Rain, sweat and tears flow together in unison. Making my way across 1000 kilometres, I concentrated solely on the centimetre in question. Then the next. In a corridor, passing through the unknown. Back home, I'm familiar with a maelstrom of different paths, each more or less comfortable, but with this, I've burst right out of my confines. I've extended myself to reach my limits, pushing them back a little further. A kind of stretching exercise. But like a sneeze that's reluctant to come, I wonder if I've peaked yet. Maybe it'll happen when I rewrite this tale. When I relive it. Or maybe I'm already there.

The descent to the Swiss border is striking. As I enter my homeland, a subtle rainbow plays hard-to-get, so I stop and take a photo spattered with raindrops. My phone has finally regained its independence, so I let B1 know I'll be back in a few hours' time. We've planned a big dinner on my return. I also activate the location tracking system so my friends and family can follow me on this hairpin-bend home-straight. The rain eases off as I slip between the Brenet and de Joux lakes. Once I've passed the quaysides, I get stuck into the ascent of the Mollendruz pass, which is actually less arduous than expected. I then let myself flow down to the fields in the district of Morges, crossing the Venoge river.

Lausanne.
As I come to roads I know, I get the strange feeling that I just nipped out for some bread. I race up my hometown, upright on the pedals. This last push is the hardest of the whole trip because I'm going fast out of impatience. I'm no more than two minutes away from my goal. Climbing the final few metres, I breathe so heavily that a passer-by, living a normal day, stares at me in alarm. I must have eyes like the devil. I get to my avenue. I turn right and hurtle down it, panting like a buffalo on heat and, through my sweat-fogged contact lenses, I glimpse a small gathering outside my apartment block. A few pedal-pushes later, I recognise my mother, father, brother, and B1. My four favourite people are waiting for me with tears in their eyes and flowers in their hands. I brake when I reach them and put my feet on the ground. The questions and cries are already flying. I can see my journey springing to life in their eyes, and it begins to sizzle inside me. When I dismount my steed to hug them, I note that I don't collapse.

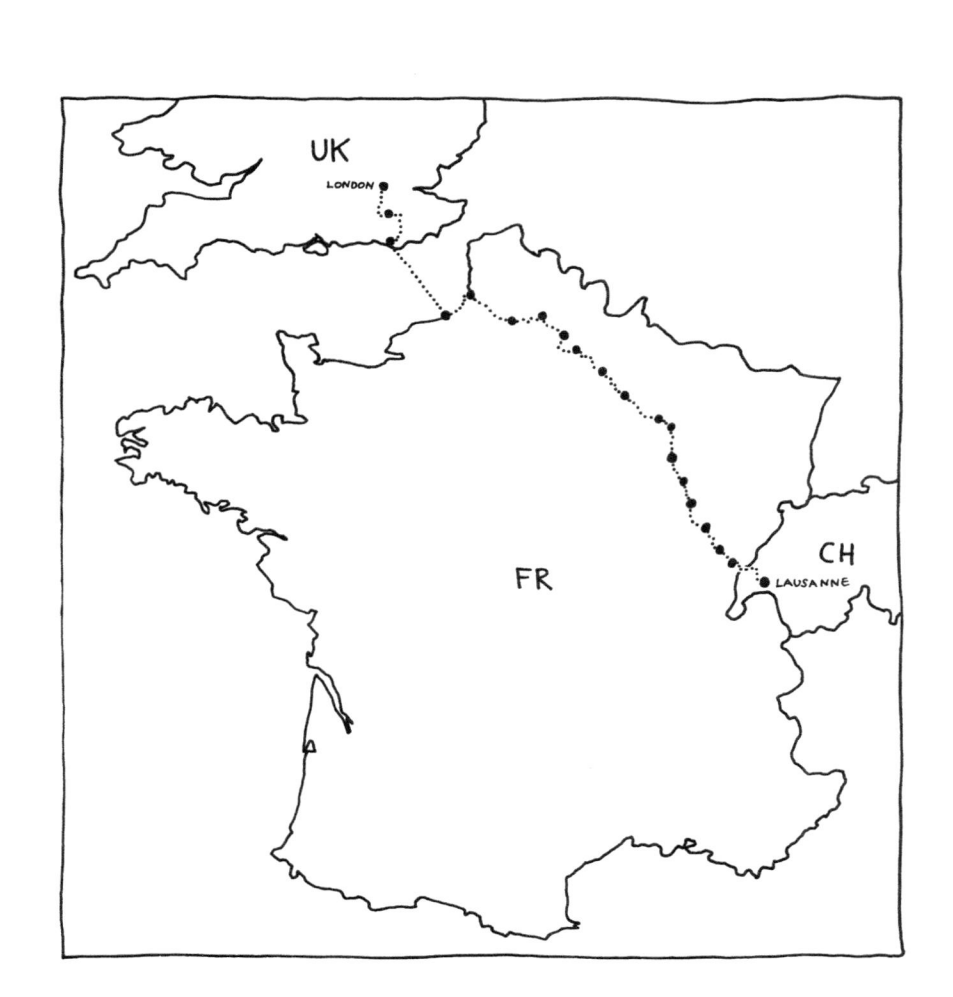

With grateful thanks

To Benni, the friend of my life, my comfort, my refuge*, for his invaluable support and without whom this would not have existed.

To my parents Jacky and Philippe, and to my brother David, for their unconditional support.

To Emmanuelle, Françoise and Deborah, my cycling confederates**, for their sympathetic ear and encouragement. To Alexia for her faith in me, and the fun little friendship that flourished following our ludicrously long *vouvoiement****. To Lynette for her patience, immense kindness and enthusiasm.

And in no particular order: to the cats I encountered throughout this trip, my family members at home and away, my cousins, uncles, aunts – including two of the 'great' variety – and Granny whose writing and travelling inspired this. To my *trois Vieilles* and Barbara (all four quite feline), the *ateliée* and its fantastic fauna, and my friends near and far (canines included).

---

* My 'comfuge'?
** My 'cycos'? Maybe not!
*** Going from the formal *vous* to the informal *tu*. Like from a handshake to a hug.

∞

BV - #0080 - 271124 - C0 - 210/148/9 - PB - 9781068540004 - Matt Lamination